The Illinois and Michigan Canal

A Contemporary Perspective in Essays and Photographs

Jim Redd

Southern Illinois University Press
Carbondale and Edwardsville

Library of Congress Cataloging-in-Publication Data

Redd, Jim.
  The Illinois and Michigan Canal : a contemporary perspective in
essays and photographs / Jim Redd.
      p.   cm.
    1. Illinois and Michigan Canal National Heritage Corridor (Ill.)
2. Illinois and Michigan Canal National Heritage Corridor (Ill.)—
Pictorial works.   3. Illinois and Michigan Canal (Ill.)
4. Illinois and Michigan Canal (Ill.)—Pictorial works.   I. Title.
F547.I13R44   1993
977.3'2—dc20   91-22200
ISBN 0-8093-1660-9   CIP

Frontispiece: Lock chamber wall detail showing wear
from canal boats

For Marshia

If a channel were cut through this ridge, one could sail from Lake Illinois to the Sea of Florida.
—Jacques Marquette, 1673

Contents

Photographs   xi
Map   facing pages xiv–xv
Acknowledgments   xvii

Essays

Introduction: The Canal   1
Plate. Railroad Tie Path Across the Canal, East of Utica   xx

The Portage   7
Plate. The Chicago Portage   6

The Summit Division   9
Plate. Site of the Canal Junction with the Chicago River   10

The Locks   13
Plate. Lock 2 Downstream Entry Bay, West of Lockport   14

The Aqueducts   17
Plate. Aqueduct over Nettle Creek, Gebhard Woods, Morris   16

Leo   19
Plate. Canal Bed from the Columbus Street Bridge, Ottawa   20

Dresden   27
Plate. Site of Dresden, Grundy County   26

Contents

Marquette   31
Plate. Cross Marking Marquette's Winter Stay in Chicago   32

Mount Forest Island   37
Plate. Saganashkee Slough, South of Mount Forest Island   36

The *City of Pekin*   45
Plate. Keel of the City of Pekin *in Dry Canal Bed,
Channahon*   46

Buffalo Rock   51
*Plate. Outcropping of Limestone and Overlying Pennsylvanian
Coal, Buffalo Rock*   50

"Irish Rebellion"   53
Plate. Dry Canal Bed, Between Utica and La Salle   54

The Western Division   57
Plate. Lock 12, West of Ottawa   58

Photographs begin on page 68

x

Photographs

1. Lock 2 chamber, looking west, west of Lockport   68
2. Lock 2, north wall, tail bay, west of Lockport   69
3. The Chicago Portage   70
4. The canal between Utica and La Salle   71
5. The I&M Canal at midsummer, between Utica and La Salle   72
6. The canal, looking east, in the Gebhard Woods State Park, Morris   73
7. Unocal Oil Refinery, near Lemont   74
8. Lockport pumping station of the Wolverine Pipeline Company   75
9. Tank farm near the site of the Chicago Portage   76
10. Tank farm near the site of the Chicago Portage   77
11. Brandon Lock on the Illinois Waterway, Joliet   78
12. Lock 10, Marseilles   79
13. Lock 9, Marseilles   80
14. Lock 14, La Salle, looking west   81
15. Lock 14, chamber and mitre gate, La Salle   82
16. Lock 14, gate detail, showing heavy balance beam, La Salle   83
17. Aqueduct over the Little Vermillion River, La Salle   84
18. Fox River Aqueduct, looking east, Ottawa   85
19. Aqueduct over Aux Sable Creek, Grundy County   86
20. Railroad bed, looking east, between La Salle and Utica   87
21. Looking southwest from the Kingery Road bridge   88
22. Illinois Central Railroad trestle, near La Salle   89
23. Iron ring for docking canal boats on the Norton Building, Lockport   90
24. St. Patrick's Church, La Salle   91
25. Restored barn, adjacent to the side cut, Ottawa   92
26. House on the canal bank, La Salle   93

27. Canal-era facades, Canal Street, Lemont   94
28. Gaylord Building, Lockport   95
29. Reddick Mansion, Ottawa   96
30. The "Halfway House," between Joliet and Chicago   97
31. Grain elevator, Seneca   98
32. Canal-era barn, Dresden   99
33. St. James Sag Church, Mount Forest Island   100
34. St. James Sag Cemetery, Mount Forest Island   101
35. Père Marquette monument, Summit   102
36. Père Marquette monument, Utica   103
37. Towpath, near DuPage River slackwater crossing, Channahon   104
38. Strip mine tailings, Buffalo Rock   105
39. Cog Hill Golf Course   106
40. Gravel quarry, near Utica   107
41. Limestone kiln ruins, Blackball Mines, near Utica   108
42. Limestone kiln ruins, Blackball Mines, near Utica   109
43. The "bottoms," along the canal, near La Salle   110
44. Carey Marsh, Illinois River bottomlands north of the canal, near Utica   111
45. The "bottoms," looking north toward the Illinois River   112
46. Split Rock, the canal, and its towpath, looking southwest   113

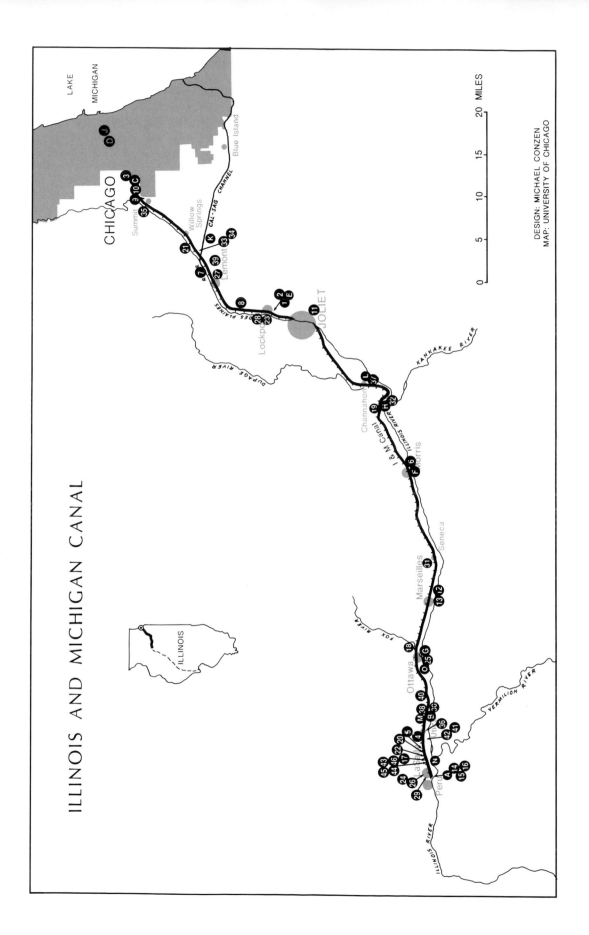

ILLINOIS AND MICHIGAN CANAL

DESIGN: **MICHAEL CONZEN**
MAP: UNIVERSITY OF CHICAGO

The numbers and letters on the map identify the approximate location where each photograph appearing in the book was taken. The numbers correspond to the plate numbers of the photographs beginning on page 68. The letters refer to the unnumbered photographs. "A" shows the location of the jacket front illustration; the remaining letters (B–O) refer to the photographs appearing at the beginning of each essay as follows:

MAP KEY	PLATE NAME	PAGE NO.
B	Railroad tie path across the canal, east of Utica	xx
C	The Chicago portage	6
D	Site of the canal junction with the Chicago River	10
E	Lock 2 downstream entry bay, west of Lockport	14
F	Aqueduct over Nettle Creek, Gebhard Woods, Morris	16
G	Canal bed from the Columbus Street bridge, Ottawa	20
H	Site of Dresden, Grundy County	26
J	Cross marking Marquette's winter stay in Chicago	32
K	Saganashkee Slough, south of Mount Forest Island	36
L	Keel of the *City of Pekin* in dry canal bed, Channahon	46
M	Outcropping of limestone and overlying Pennsylvanian coal, Buffalo Rock	50
N	Dry canal bed, between Utica and La Salle	54
O	Lock 12, west of Ottawa	58

Acknowledgments

Had I not met, by chance, David Bolaños at the Busy Bee Restaurant in early May of 1986, this book would have never been written. He told me of his recent canoe trip down something called the "I&M Canal," which I had never heard of, despite my ten years residence in Chicago. Once I started on the project, there were many others who offered information, assistance, and criticism.

My next fortunate encounter was with Philip Vierling, high school teacher and local geologist par excellence. For most of the geological information in this book I am indebted to his *Hiking the Illinois and Michigan Canal and Exploring Its Environs*, a wonderfully detailed field guide to the western part of the corridor.

No one knows the history of the canal better than John Lamb of Lewis University, and I wish to thank him for sharing it with me and for making available the canal archives at that university (and for the last-minute fax of a badly needed map!). In particular, I am indebted to him for most of the factual information in the *City of Pekin* chapter.

Another important resource was the exhaustive index of *The Illinois and Michigan Canal* by Michael Kontzen of The University of Chicago. I also appreciate the assistance given by the staffs of the Chicago Historical Society, the Field Museum of Natural History, the Newberry Library, the La Salle County Historical Society at Utica, and the Chicago Public Library.

For encouragement in the project, I wish to thank Jerry Adelmann of the Canal Corridor Association, Carter Manny of the Graham Foundation, Larry Viskochil of the Chicago Historical Society, Cheryl Hahn of the Illinois State Museum at Lockport, and especially Henry Tabor of Kroch's and Brentano's bookstore in Chicago.

Sylvia Lewis got me off to the right start by editing early manuscripts, and Richard DeBacher of Southern Illinois University

Press gave me further guidance in this regard. Bill O'Donnell also helped with the editing.

Mrs. Herbert Stevenson and Leo Rossitor of Ottawa and Mr. Dollinger of Dresden were gracious enough to give me some of their time, and I have them to thank for adding a human dimension to the book.

Thanks to Steve Greiner, photographer, for the use of his camera equipment, to Jane Wenger for help in organizing the photographs, to Deborah Zajac for her assistance with the map, to Carol Hester for her help in proofreading, and to the National Park Service for helping with the finances by purchasing some of my prints.

Essays

Railroad ties laid as a path across the canal, east of Utica. *Western Division, Mile 89, El. 471 ft. (109 ft. below lake level)*

Introduction: The Canal

Let us bind the Republic together with a perfect system of roads and canals.

—John C. Calhoun, 1817

The Illinois and Michigan Canal was the first great public works project undertaken in the upper Midwest, and one of the last of the many transportation canals built in this country in the nineteenth century. Its construction began in 1836, and when completed in 1848, the canal was the final link in a continuous water route from the East to the Gulf of Mexico via the Erie Canal, the Great Lakes, and the Illinois and Mississippi river systems.

Its route lay from the Chicago River at Bridgeport, now a neighborhood on Chicago's southwest side, to the Illinois River at La Salle, Illinois, a hundred miles to the southwest. The physical dimensions were modest compared with other canals: 40 feet wide at the water level, 28 feet wide at the bottom (a "prism" shape), with a 6-foot water depth. The 150-foot difference in water level between Lake Michigan and the Illinois River at La Salle was controlled by sixteen locks. In addition to the locks, there were twenty-five bridges across the canal, four aqueducts for crossing streams and rivers, four "feeders" for supplying water to the canal from rivers, and a number of dams. The construction materials were timber, stone, and mortar, and the tools were picks and shovels.

For the first six years of its operation, before the first railroad was laid along its path in 1854, the canal enjoyed a virtual monopoly on trade between the Mississippi Valley and the East. Previously, goods had been either shipped through New Orleans or carried in wagons on overland trails; the prices in both regions reflected the high cost of shipping. The new through route lowered and leveled the

1

prices for both eastern merchandise and Midwest farm produce, and as these effects rippled through the heartland, families and businesses began to reorient themselves; the impact of the canal was felt in almost every aspect of economic activity.

Because of the reduced shipping costs, corn became the most profitable crop of the prairies and wheat production was almost abandoned. Cheaper salt from the salines of western New York encouraged stock raising. There was a general shift from reliance on items produced locally with materials at hand to dependence on trade goods from remote sources. Stores became stocked with cheaper merchandise from Chicago, permanently diminishing the commercial hegemony of St. Louis in the region. From the southern plantations moved barges piled high with bales of cotton and hogsheads of sugar, molasses, and tobacco. White pine from Michigan penciled through the canal in huge quantities, resulting in the abandonment of local sawmills. It was no longer necessary to build log cabins and rough-hewn fences, barns, and furniture from the scarce timber found in groves and along the streams and rivers. The excavation of the canal bed had revealed rich veins of limestone, sandstone, gravel, and clay, upon which grew numerous quarrying and mining industries.

But the most obvious beneficiary of the canal trade was Chicago, whose first recorded business was the sale of canal lots for construction capital. Its population grew from twelve hundred when canal construction began, to seventy-four thousand after six years of operation, a boom due largely to its location as a cargo transfer point between lake and canal boats. Chicago continued to grow throughout the canal era: in 1879, a typical year, over seven million bushels of grain, forty million feet of lumber, sixty thousand barrels of flour and salt, and forty-three cubic yards of quarry stone moved across its wharves.

The decades between 1860 and 1890 were the peak years of cargo traffic on the canal. During this period more than five million tons of freight were transported generating a million dollars in tolls. These were years of heavy immigration and intense economic activity—years in which the foundation was laid for the future of the region. The character and flavor of life in the upper Midwest today is a legacy of the era of the Illinois and Michigan Canal.

As the Midwest moved toward industrialization, the capacity of the canal became inadequate to accommodate the increased shipping demands, and the railroads became ascendant. Use of the canal declined rapidly after the turn of the century, when a larger waterway, the Sanitary and Ship Canal, partially replaced it, and in 1933 it was formally closed to navigation. The I&M Canal dried up and was forgotten as modern travel and commerce turned to the railroads, larger canals, and then the highways. In the last fifty years its prism has become overgrown and segmented, its stone locks gradually deteriorating.

When I first came upon one of the locks, I was reminded of ancient Roman ruins or entangled monoliths in the forests of the Yucatan. I remember, as I stood on the rough stone edge looking down into the chamber, my sadness that such classic work had not been preserved. The side walls were weathered mosaics of precisely cut and fitted limestone, indented with the scrapes, gouges, and grooves of hundreds of canal boats. Tree roots, growing through the joints of the masonry, had forced fragments into the shallow stream trickling through the canal bed. To my left and right, the long, narrow chamber flared out at each end to form the entry bays, the walls curving out and tapering downward in pleasing proportion and symmetry. On the other side of the lock, I could see a smooth rounded lip—an engraved molding—running the length of the lock along the top edge of the wall showing a refinement and a care for detail beyond mere function. But what I remember most about that lock, and what inspired me to explore and photograph the others, was the puzzle of its appeal: why did I find such value in something so decrepit and devoid of purpose?

By the time I had photographed all the locks, I had carried my large camera behind junkyards, under and across rusting railroad trestles, along weedy, little-used paths through litter-strewn backlots, around abandoned quarries and the rusting ruins of twentieth-century industry. The stench of stagnant water and industrial waste frequently filled the air. In the bottoms, mosquitos swarmed with a ferocity unchanged since the days of canal construction. But the reality of this unmoderated harshness was engaging in its own way, and I have made no effort to disguise it in the photographs. The contrast of this landscape, which persistently etched itself on my film, with that described by Marquette and other early travelers, was unavoidable, and I came to view the canal from another perspective—as the precursor to the industrialization that has left so little of the natural beauty of the land undisturbed. My admiration for Yankee ingenuity and foresight represented by the canal began to cool as I contemplated the sterile, acid-ridden soil of strip mine tailings, or the polluted water of a channelized Des Plaines River. Even the abandoned mines seemed symbols of our insatiable need to exploit, consume, and then move onto another vein. As a traveler through Illinois wrote in 1833, "The works of man are mere distortions compared with those of nature."[1]

Nature's bequest to the Midwest was a topography built up of long periods of submersion below tropical seas and subsequent elevations, evidenced by layers of clay, silt, and sand between those of limestone. A million years ago, the surface signature was the result of the ebb and flow of these ancient seas. Then began the glacial assault from the North that all but erased this surface record—grinding, leveling, and reshaping the landscape—burying it under a mile of moving ice. Moraines were piled up around the edges of its lobes, forming interglacial lakes that filled to overflow, then drained through enormous sluiceways. The erosive power of these torrents bared once more the buried veins of minerals, making them accessible to later human exploitation. By two thousand years ago, the outflows had subsided and settled to their valley floors, the climate had moderated, and the moraines and valleys were becoming forested: the geography described in the journals and letters of the first European travelers.

The writings of Marquette contain the earliest reference to the valley formed by one of those meltwater surges. It drained glacial Lake Chicago, across which the city now spreads, through the Des Plaines and Illinois river valleys. The channel left by this flow had been used for centuries as a trade route by native Americans, and later by the French explorers, traders, and missionaries traveling between the Great Lakes and the interior settlements. The I&M Canal followed this same route.

The structures in these photographs are some of the oldest in the Midwest, and I am pleased to have "rescued" them photographically

---

[1] Paul M. Angle, ed., *Prairie State: Impressions of Illinois, 1673–1967, by Travellers and Other Observers* (Chicago: The University of Chicago Press, 1968), p. 133.

from further deterioration. As I became more intrigued with the era in which they were built, I began to gather related written and oral material from which emerged the accompanying text. It is meant to reach beyond the surface textures and arrangement of things, to give depth and illuminate ideas latent in the thin silver image of the photographs. Some of these essays are purely descriptive, based on facts from my research. But as I became more familiar with the corridor, I began to consider historical fact as a starting point, only relevant insofar as it enhanced my understanding and sensitivity to the landscape as it is today. Therefore, this book reflects that intimacy by expressing some of my personal experience and thoughts, poised against the objective detail of the photographs.

This book should not be considered a comprehensive study or history of the canal. There are many books and much factual material on the subject. I have excluded some sections of the canal, either because they were inaccessible, they were not interesting photographically, or I just did not get to them for whatever reason. Other sections are treated with much detail. I was guided primarily by intuition, and I explored areas that appealed to me or that seemed special or interesting.

The remains of the canal represent the final flourish of a preindustrial technology, basically unchanged for more than a thousand years, and recall an era when men approached the natural landscape with less technical ability, if not more humility, than today. As modern technology continues to intrude upon the land, I offer in this book a reconsideration of the values of simple elegance and craftsmanship embodied by the Illinois and Michigan Canal.

The Chicago Portage

The Portage

The mud was very deep, and along the edge of the lake grew tall grass and wild rice, often above a man's head, and so strong and dense it was almost impossible to walk through them. Those who waded through the mud frequently sank to their waist, and at times were forced to cling to the side of the boat to prevent going over their heads. [They] suffered great agony, their limbs becoming swollen and enflamed, and their sufferings were not ended for two or three days. It took us three consecutive days of toil to pass all our boats through this miserable lake.
—G. Saltonstall Hubbard, 1818, the first American
to record his Mud Lake crossing

Encircling the southern shore of Lake Michigan, a few miles beyond the shoreline dunes, is an upland border of modest height that separates the lake basin from the interior valleys. Within this narrow collar, water drains into the lake and eventually empties into the St. Lawrence River on the other side, rivers flow toward the Mississippi River and the Gulf of Mexico.

These watercourses were followed by early traders and adventurers in their expeditions into the hinterland. They coasted south along either the eastern or western shore of the lake, and entered one of its rivers. After paddling to the headwaters, they portaged their canoes and goods across the low divide to a tributary of an inland river, and descended southwest.

One of the earliest routes was from Green Bay to the Illinois River by way of the Fox River, across what is now central Wisconsin. It was used by fur traders and missionaries in the latter half of the seventeenth century and was the portage from which Marquette and Joliet began their 1673 voyage down the Mississippi. On their return from this trip, they were told by the Illinois Indians of another, shorter route that joined Lake Michigan south of Green Bay. Canoeing up the Illinois to the Des Plaines, they followed the Des Plaines almost to its headwaters, then portaged east to the lake. Thereafter, this new route began appearing on maps as the "Chicago Portage," and ultimately became the most important of the mid-continental gateways.

If one thinks of Lake Michigan as an index finger buried knuckle-deep in the American pie, pointing toward New Orleans, a slight flick has raised a low ridge an eighth of an inch from the nail. A toothpick trace—the Des Plaines River—begins near the cuticle and meanders along the ridge until it spills away from the tip into the Illinois Valley to the southwest. This eighth of an inch was the shortest overland leg of all the portages, and Marquette was the first to suggest a connecting "channel" be dug.

But nature's toll for this geographic shortcut was seven miles of muddy misery. Between the Des Plaines and the lake was a swampy lowland, usually too shallow to paddle and too deep to wade—a puddle from the Pleistocene. Ten thousand years before, this portage, and the entire lake plain, was the bottom of Lake Michigan's glacial ancestor, Lake Chicago. Its gradual withdrawal left this swamp astride the subcontinental divide, fed one day by water from the lake, the next from the Des Plaines River. In seasons of heavy rainfall, waters destined for the Gulf of Mexico mingled with the mud of those that would wash across the ridge to the Mississippi.

Symbolically, the swamp was also a watershed—a physical link—bridging the natural history of the glaciers, recently retreated to the east, with the written history of the Americans, now advancing to the west. To them it became infamous as "Mud Lake." During the forty years centered at the beginning of the nineteenth century, they sloshed back and forth across it with their canoes, wagons, and horses, establishing the eastern connection of the route that would culminate in the "channel" envisioned by Marquette 250 years before: the Illinois and Michigan Canal.

The Summit Division

Rivers are ungovernable things, especially in Hilly country. Canals are quiet and very manageable.
—Ben Franklin, 1772

During the spring and early summer of 1836, William Gooding, chief engineer for the canal project, and his staff began surveying for the exact location of the canal. They had to determine the length of each reach, compute the depths and widths throughout the course, decide where aqueducts and locks would be necessary, and calculate the lift of each lock. For construction and later administrative purposes, the project was divided into three divisions: The Summit Division, between the Chicago River and Lockport; the Middle Division, between Lockport and Seneca; and the Western Division, from Seneca to the terminus at La Salle.

The first section surveyed was the Summit Division. Its actual connection with the Chicago River was made in the south fork of the south branch, just south of the present Ashland Avenue bridge. Although this part of the canal has long since been covered over, the clump of trees in the photograph (p. 10), looking north on Ashland Avenue, shrouds the shoreline indentation of the old canal river junction.

From the river, the canal was dug southwestward, across Ashland Avenue. Near Wood Street, two blocks away, a Y was formed between the canal itself and a short, dead-end section that extended toward, but did not connect with, the river. This section provided docking and loading facilities.

It continued southwest across Damen Avenue at Thirtieth Street. From Hoyne Avenue southwest, Bross Avenue was laid out parallel to the canal. From Leavitt and Thirty-first Street, it followed

9

Site of the canal junction with the Chicago River, Twenty-seventh Street and Ashland Avenue, Chicago. *Summit Division, Mile 0, El. 580 ft. (lake level)*

the route that the Stevenson Expressway now occupies as far as Harlem Avenue.

The bottom of the canal was to be dug at lake level across the old Lake Chicago bottom, around the southern shore of Mud Lake, and through the eight-foot ridge, allowing water to flow freely from the river, across the divide, and down the canal. For the first seven miles the workers dug easily into the soft silt and clay of the lake plain—from which would come "Chicago Common" brick used to rebuild after the fire—but as they neared the divide, their shovels clanged into hard bedrock. They had unexpectedly struck the top of the layer of Niagaran dolomite that underlies the Great Lakes basins and most of the Midwest.

It is surprising that an engineer of William Gooding's experience would not have known about this strata, since it outcrops along the banks of the Des Plaines River, only a few miles from where the canal was being dug. Once I walked along the levee that now restrains the river from reclaiming its vestigial bed to the lake. I followed a trail down toward the bank where a recent flooding had spread a uniform layer of dark brown silt and mud. Beneath the mud the molded shapes of cans, bottles, and tires were outlined. White plastic bags billowed and twisted from the mud-caked twigs of small trees, and the air was tinged with chemical pungency. The mud adhered in clumps and tugged at my boots. I pushed aside the branches of trees lining the river and stepped from the ooze onto a hard shelf an inch beneath the surface of the water. Mud streamed from my boots, thinning downstream.

The rock was flat and extended about thirty feet along the bank; I could see that it continued across the river, reappearing on the far bank. Its jagged serrations protruded from the 5,000-foot-thick slab of dolomite. Although not strictly "bedrock," it is effectively the basement floor of the Midwest, having been laid down in the Silurian period. For the next four hundred million years, layer upon layer of softer sediment accumulated from succeeding shallow seas. The final layer settled from glacial Lake Chicago during the last fourteen thousand years of the Pleistocene. Two thousand years ago, the lake receded, leaving the Des Plaines River coursing across the former lake bottom, back through those amassed sediments, eroding them one by one, until it reached and revealed once more this resistant dolomite. It was surprisingly brittle, and with the toe of my boot I easily broke off a thin wafer and sent it spinning beneath the surface.

The canal workers had to use picks to break this gray rock into shovel-sized chunks, and progress toward the summit slowed almost to a standstill until it became clear that the "deep cut" through the summit was not practical. The design was changed to include a lock and pumping station—called the Santa Fe Slip—at the site of the shrimp shop, shown on p. 10. The pump lifted boats eight feet above the bedrock and over the summit level. Because of the slight gradient, this level was maintained for thirty miles, following the Des Plaines River through Lemont to Lock 1 at Lockport, where the 150-foot fall to the Illinois River began.

The Locks

The locks and abutments are laid in smooth, handsome
masonry that would do no discredit to any part of our country.
                                                   —J. H. Buckingham, 1847

Certainly, even today, one of the most satisfying aspects of
the canal locks is their uniformity in proportion, materials, and
craftsmanship. When compared with their modern successors, the
old locks present a pleasing sense of scale, quietly preserving the
handmade quality of nineteenth-century technology.

The locks and gates were all constructed from one common plan
and set of specifications, the dimensions being 110 feet long by 18
feet wide inside the chamber, with a depth depending on the amount
of lift. There is evidence that the chief engineer, William Gooding,
following common engineering practice, modified existing lock and
gate plans from other canals in the East, rather than develop a set of
completely original designs for the I&M Canal. Regardless of the
source of the designs, it appears that Mr. Gooding, in applying them
to the actual conditions of this project, accepted nothing less than
the highest quality in the materials and construction of the locks and
in the manufacture and installation of the gates.

The pound lock, so called because it "impounded" the water
between two gates, was first used in China in the tenth century, a
thousand years before the invention of the transportation canal in
Egypt. Pound locks, using vertically rising gates, were built in
Europe in the fourteenth century. The swinging, or mitre gate, used
in the I&M Canal, was invented by Leonardo da Vinci in the late
fifteenth century. The inspiration and major source of canal technology and design expertise to America was Great Britain, where a
"Canal Age" flourished in the last half of the eighteenth century.

Lock 2 downstream entry bay, west of Lockport. *Middle Division, Mile 30, El. 570 ft. (10 ft. below lake level), Lift 10 ft.*

The lock system of the I&M Canal maintained a navigable water level between the Chicago River at Lake Michigan and the Illinois River at La Salle. A canal boat traveling from Chicago was first raised eight feet by the pumping station at the Chicago River and was maintained at that level for thirty miles across the summit. From there, the boat descended 150 feet through fifteen locks to the level of the Illinois River, ninety miles to the southwest. Each lock lowered the boat between eight and fifteen feet.

The locks were numbered from east to west, Lock 1 being in Lockport. The first lock, at the Chicago River, was not necessary in the first "deep cut" plan and thus was not included in the numbering system.

Lock 9, near Chicago and Pearl streets in Marseilles, is shown in plates 12 and 13. Although Marseilles is thought of as a "canal town," it was actually settled in the 1820s near rapids on the Illinois River that proved useful as a source of power for milling and other industries. The town was surveyed in 1835, a year before the groundbreaking of the canal, but the original plat shows no evidence of the canal that would cut across the town site twelve years later.

Lock 14 in La Salle was restored to its original operational condition in 1979 by the Illinois Department of Conservation, which has maintained the canal since 1954 (plates 14, 15, and 16). The narrow restriction beyond the gate in plate 14, looking west toward the river, is the site of Lock 15. This lock separated the steamboat basin, at river level, from the canal boat basin, where the transfer of cargo and passengers took place between river and canal vessels.

Aqueduct over Nettle Creek, Gebhard Woods, Morris. *Middle Division, Mile 57, El. 508 ft. (72 ft. below lake level)*

The Aqueducts

Beauty seems to result from perfect fitness.
—Charles S. Whitney, 1929

The Illinois and Michigan Canal followed the natural drainage path of northeastern Illinois, crossing the channels of major tributaries of the Illinois River, several creeks, and numerous small streams. Water flow from the streams was either accepted into the canal or routed underneath through culverts. But neither of these methods was suitable for the larger creeks and rivers, which required the construction of aqueducts.

The longest was the four-hundred-foot limestone and timber aqueduct over the Fox River north of Ottawa (plate 18). Similar constructions were used for the Aux Sable and Nettle creeks in Grundy County, and the Little Vermillion River at La Salle, just before the termination point at the Illinois River.

The canal route crossed the DuPage River near Channahon. Here, the respective water levels prohibited the use of an aqueduct, so an ancient method called slack pool navigation was employed. A dam or weir was built just downstream of the point of crossing, and locks were located on each side of the river. A tow bridge was built over the river between the locks, allowing the canal boats to be towed across the river in the slack pool created by the dam.

Dealing with the existing natural waterways that the canal crossed was a significant challenge to the canal engineers. In fact, the precise location of the canal route between Joliet and La Salle was almost completely determined by the placement of the aqueducts: each one had to be high enough to provide a sufficient waterway below for natural drainage at flood stage, but low enough to maintain the correct gradient for the canal.

17

Plates 17 and 19 show that the original timber construction has been replaced by steel, but the original stonework supports remain. The house in the distance, southwest of the Aux Sable aqueduct (plate 19), was the home of the tender for Lock 8.

The Little Vermillion River aqueduct (plate 17) is shown looking southwest, with the Chicago Burlington and Quincy Railroad trestle over the Illinois River in the distance. This aqueduct is located a quarter mile from the confluence of the Little Vermillion River with the Illinois River, and about three-quarters of a mile west of Lock 14 at La Salle.

The photograph on page 16 shows the only stone arch aqueduct on the canal. It crosses Nettle Creek near Morris in Gebhard Woods, a patch of lush greenery watered by runoff from the canal itself.

Leo

Nowadays, kids don't know a feeder from a sidecut.
                                    —Leo Rossitor, 1990

It is December, and Leo and I are leaning on the rail of the Columbus Street bridge in Ottawa, looking down at the canal bed. At one time it was thought that the western terminus of the canal would be in Ottawa, and the town was officially established by the canal commissioners in 1829 as the counterpart to its "sister city," Chicago. The streets were laid out in reference to the canal, but now it looks like a sunken back alley running through the middle of town.

I took the photograph on page 20 in July, from the same spot where Leo and I are standing. Except for this one pond, the canal bed was completely dry. Now, children are ice-skating in circles on the frozen surface, forming a line, single file, then breaking up and scattering like pop beads toward the edges. I can hear their shrill cries and laughter. A spike of winter sunlight glints across Leo's face, reflected from one of the blades. "Sometimes we would skate clear to Marseilles, and take the Interurban back late at night," he says. "Once we even made a iceboat with sails, and let the wind blow us along the canal. That was somethin', jus' lay back and let the wind blow us right down that canal."

Leo Rossitor was born a half block from the I&M Canal Fox River aqueduct, in a small frame house at the end of Superior Street in Ottawa in 1901. His father had emigrated from County Wexford and his mother from County Mayo in Ireland. They were married in Ottawa in 1887, and his father started working in a brick factory, making firebrick to be shipped up the canal to build the blast furnaces in Joliet and Gary. "Back in them days, this was all solid Irish," Leo says. And it was here, south of the canal, that his father

19

Canal bed from the Columbus Street bridge, Ottawa. *Western Division, Mile 81, El. 491 ft. (89 ft. below lake level)*

built the house where Leo still lives—alone and childless—the last of a family of five. "On the other side of the canal were the Cariaris, the O'Briens, and the O'Connors," he says.

From Leo's front yard, where I met him this morning, I could see the old aqueduct crossing the river down at the end of his street, a plain, black iron trough angling straight across the tops of the original seven limestone pillars.

"I used to hear the canal boats whistle during the night from my bed as they come to the river crossing," Leo says. "My older brother worked unloading barges just across the river there—timber, them big twelve by twenty-four's from Chicago. I was the waterboy. Made $1.50 a day, and that was plenty back then. In them days, that aqueduct [he pronounces it 'ay-kee-dok'] was all timber."

I look back at the aqueduct. The iron conduit seems out of place—a twentieth-century graft on a nineteenth-century design; it does not fit the original grooves on the piers and the seven seem excessive when, with iron, two would do. I think of the grace and beauty of the Roman aqueducts, built of limestone without mortar. Whether or not the original Fox River aqueduct was reminiscent of those ancient structures, its strength was impressive: imagine a wooden construction, regardless of its form, that could hold more than sixteen hundred tons of water, two mules, and a canal boat.

Leo wants to describe how the workers repaired the timbers of the "ay-kee-dok" superstructure. He gestures, as in charades, to give voice to images and impressions clear as crystal in his own mind after seventy years, but which shatter and fragment on the hard brink of speech.

A green baseball cap, a quarter-size too big, rests in his earslots. A purple plaid sweater hangs from his slight frame. He walks lightly, his thin, bowed legs springing outward inside his black corduroy pants. His oblong ears seem to have outgrown his other features, and his brows are like serifs above the dots of his eyes, which are now following the skaters in their patterns on the ice.

I ask him about the bridges opening for the canal boats. One part of that bridge mechanism grabbed Leo's attention seventy years ago and still hasn't let loose: something he calls a "dog."

I say, "Leo, did these bridges open up and down or sideways?" Leo says, "Well, they opened in a circle-like, and they was thishere 'dog,' you see, that would lock the bridge in place."

"How many men did it take to open a bridge?"

"They was, I think, one—he pushed on a long pole, and when it was open, they was thishere dog . . ."

He uses his knuckles—they are surprisingly smooth, like aged ivory—to show me how the interlocking device worked as we walk down the towpath toward La Salle Street. We pass a small one-room building, a barber shop, which Leo says was once the toll-taker's booth for the canal boats. (There were two other booths: one in Lockport and one at the eastern end of the canal in Chicago.)

One of the skaters, a boy about twelve years old, recognizes Leo. He separates from the string and careens toward us like a crippled bat, legs outspread and arms waving in the air. "Hi, Mr. Rossiter," he yells, as the blades of his skates slice into the soft, black mud at the edge of the ice. The others laugh as he falls facedown in the damp weeds. Leo and I give him a hand and a shove back out onto the ice.

At La Salle Street, Leo scrapes the mud from his boots onto the curb.

"They was a bridge here, too. When we heard the whistle from the canal boat, us kids would hide from the tender and swing out, hanging below the bridge, danglin' our feet in that cool canal water. From there, I could get a good look at 'at there dog and see how it worked from below."

He raises his two hands, knuckles interlocked, above his head, to give me the view from underneath, moving the middle finger of one hand in the V of the other. But from the palmside, it suggests something other than that dog, and despite his age, Leo looks at me and grins like an adolescent.

After lunch, Leo takes me to the end of Canal Street, where it meets the dry bed. He shows me stone abutments, the only remaining feature of the guard lock for the "side cut," a lateral canal that ran seven blocks through town to a hydraulic basin then drained through a mill race into the Fox River. We walk down Canal Street to Lincoln Place where the basin was.

"This was the whole width of it. You wouldn't believe it unless you seen it. And in the winter, all them boats crowded in here, tied up waitin' for spring. The water ran under the streetcar barn and made electricity in there."

We are walking across a parking lot at the foot of La Salle Street. To the southeast is the junction of the Fox with the Illinois River. Leo sweeps his hand through the air, pointing to a low rise surrounding the lot just behind the curb.

"You can still see the old bank of the canal there," he says. "But in '33, after the canal closed, they let it dry up and we covered all this in with tile and dirt. Got five days work myself when my name was drawed from the jar."

Then Leo remembers "the feeder," and I try to remember my notes on canal history. The original canal design called for a "deep cut" at lake level across the eight-foot divide at the summit, which would have allowed an unlimited supply of lake water to flow by gravity down the lower reaches of the canal. But limestone bedrock was struck unexpectedly and by 1843 it had become apparent that the expense of digging such a deep ditch was too great, and the plan was changed to lift boats over the summit with locks, using steam-driven paddle-pumps to supply water from the Chicago River. With the loss of free-flowing lake water, it became necessary to supply the canal with water from rivers along the route. The technique was to run a "feeder" canal from somewhere upstream, at an elevation high enough to cause the water to flow down into the canal. There were four of these feeders, and one of them ran five miles from upstream on the Fox River into the canal here at Ottawa.

We get in the car and Leo directs me through town. Ottawa seems to have more than its share of historical street pairs: we cross Lincoln Place, then Douglas Street (they held a debate here in 1858), Post Street, and Paul Street. (Colonel Justus Post and Rene Paul were hired by the state to survey the canal route in 1824. Although there were four other surveys done, the "Post and Paul" map remains one of the most significant of the canal documents.) North of the canal are Marquette Street and Joliet Street (the French priest/explorer pair). There are some great stand-alones, too. DeWitt Clinton, "Father of the Erie Canal," is enstreeted, appropriately, a block from the obligatory Canal Street. The next is named for Robert Cavelier de La Salle who had envisioned a heartland empire; had his ambitions been realized, this town would be part of New France, and the three mainstreet staples—Jefferson, Madison, and Jackson—would be otherwise named. (Madison recommended construction of the canal but Monroe believed that publicly funded internal improvements were unconstitutional. The Post and Paul map, submitted during his administration, was "lost," causing a delay while another survey was conducted. It was found among files of the War Department in 1933. Monroe is notably unrepresented in Ottawa's street scheme. Canal construction was finally begun during Jackson's administration.)

Leo and I drive past the little league field and turn at a Dairy Queen onto a rutted county road. After about three miles, Leo says "Thishere's Lyman's Mound, where the feeder went into the river. They tell me they got electricity up here now. During the depression everybody come up here to dig coal. Can't see none of it now, though."

The dirt road climbs gradually between the dry bed of the feeder on the left, laced with motorcycle trails, and the half-frozen Fox River. Below the road on the river plain are tin-roofed sheds and rusting vehicles scattered among small shanties. There is a bleakness about these depression-era shacks—a need for privacy not as a temporary restorative, but that fed by suspicion and mistrust. I believe Leo when he tells me that it "ain't changed much up here since the thirties." We pass a sign: "Lefty's Landing, No Trespassing." A pickup truck passes and the driver's head swivels behind the glass like a hawk's, steady, tracking me over the bumps in the road. More unfriendly signs. I say that maybe we've come far enough, that I already know about that feeder, anyway. But Leo doesn't hear me. He is gesturing excitedly, smudging the windshield with his fingertip, pointing through the bare trees.

"Over there—see? That's where that feeder dumped into the river."

"But where was the water coming from that went into the river here, and how could it run uphill?"

He nods silently, and I realize that for more than seventy years, although he "knowed that feeder well," he has never understood that the water was flowing from the river to feed the canal, and not the other way around.

As we drive back through town, we cross the Columbus Street bridge. Now Leo remembers seeing passenger boats docked here, just where the skaters were earlier. I ask him to describe the boats, but he never got to go inside one, he says, because they were only for "rich folks." Looking east from the bridge, down the dry bed, I see low frame Monopoly houses lined along both banks of the canal. Leo tells me that those people who lived near the canal used to draw water from it for washing because it was "softer" than the mineral-laden well water.

Just before we get back to his place, Leo motions for me to stop at a house on Superior Street.

"This is where the old Fox River House was," he says.

We get out of the car and I follow him between the buildings back toward the canal.

"I remember, they was a big wooden ramp-like thing running from that towpath bank down to the hotel and if you was a driver, you could put your team up and have supper here."

Later, I look up the Fox River House in the county records. It was the second hotel in Ottawa, built in 1837, and was one of the finest along the canal. Among the names on its guest list are Abraham Lincoln, Stephen Douglas, and Daniel Webster. As canal traffic declined, so did the hotel business; by 1898 it was abandoned, and, despite Leo's recollection, was torn down in 1903, when he was only two years old.

I let Leo out of the car in front of his house. He closes the car door and stoops to look at me through the window from beneath the bill of his hat. Laying one hand across the lowered window, he says, "Well, I hope I helped you out," and grins. I look at the large, rounded knuckles of his hand, and I think that the only thing Leo knows for a fact, the only thing that he couldn't have heard from his father, or have read somewhere about this canal, or outright imagined, was how that "dog" worked on the La Salle Street Bridge. But I still haven't figured it out.

Site of Dresden, Grundy County, looking from the Minooka Ridge

Dresden

The prairies . . . their beauty and sublimity embrace every texture of soil and outline of surface, and are sufficiently undulating to prevent stagnation of water. The herbiage consists of tall grass, interspersed with flowering plants of every hue, which succeed each other as the season advances. Occasionally, clumps of trees stood on the surface, like islands in the oceans. The bounding forests projected and receded in pleasing forms, and the distant outlines appeared graceful. The wide expanse appeared the gift of God to man for the exercise of his industry.
—Patrick Shirref, 1833

This description is more poetic than most, but the feeling of awe, almost reverence, inspired by first sight of the open prairie constantly recurs in the westward chronicles. These expressions were not limited to the travel journals of European and eastern gentry; practical-minded immigrants were often moved to eloquence by the "beauty and sublimity" of the prairie.

Shirref was a Scottish farmer from East Midlothian who toured the Illinois Valley in 1833. In late August he took the Stage Road from Chicago to La Salle. Three hot, dusty days after crossing Mud Lake and the Des Plaines River, his stage approached the junction of that river with the Kankakee. Most of the trip had been along the valley floor, but now the stage rose gradually toward the crest of a hill covered with a dense growth of oak and hickory. The top was flat for perhaps half a mile, and Shirref and his companions rode in silence through the welcome coolness of the forest.

Shirref, attentive to the landscape, may have been contemplating the origin of this hill, an anomolous bulge from an otherwise flat plain, but he made no mention of it in his journal. No doubt he, like most Christians of the time, considered such large formations evidence of the hand of God and not subject to further inquiry. But the biblical version of the Flood was soon to be secularized by a Swiss geologist named Louis Agassiz: the year before he had been in Shirref's native Scotland, exploring its kames and eskers, and now he was in the Mont Blanc region of Switzerland, developing his theory of the Ice Ages. By the 1860s this new idea was being applied by geologists in America to explain the cup-shaped ridges and erratic boulders ranging across the northern states.

The hills embossing the northern Illinois landscape are now understood, thanks to Agassiz' work, to be glacial moraines. The Minooka Ridge, across which ran the Stage Road, is one of the largest, curving north to southeast. The bed of the Kankakee follows the contour of the moraine from its headwaters in Indiana to the junction with the Des Plaines. During the late Pleistocene, the paths followed by these two rivers carried a torrential outflow from the eastern and western basins, respectively, of the Great Lakes. The water they carried was embayed behind the moraine, forming a meltwater lake. When the morainal dam could no longer contain the volume of water being released from the north, it cut an overflow channel across its top that eventually eroded into a mile-wide channel. Ten thousand years later, after the flow had subsided, the channel became a natural connection point for aboriginal trails, the same route followed by the Stage Road.

When Shirref's stage emerged into the sunlight, the panorama before him may have inspired the entry in his journal. Below, to his left, were the two rivers, still joining in tribute to that ancient outflow, forming the Illinois. From its banks spread the prairie, unbroken except for the Stage Road itself and a "clump of trees" near the horizon. This was the Aux Sable timber, named after the creek that supported its growth. The stage descended the steep slope of the ridge toward the timber where the passengers would spend the night, and the coach driver would change horses at Rutherford's tavern.

After the Revolutionary War, settlers had begun moving into this part of the Illinois country, some from the South, and some from the East. Their numbers increased after the Treaty of Greenville in 1795, in which the Indians gave up large tracts of land north of the Ohio (including a six-mile-wide strip through which the I&M Canal was later dug). After the Erie Canal was completed in 1825, connecting Great Lakes steamship service was available to Chicago. The Black Hawk War of 1832 eliminated the remaining Indian claims, and immigrants began pouring in, most of them now from the East.

They believed the prairie to be untillable, and usually settled near a timber grove, which provided them with construction materials and shelter against the wind, weather, and periodic prairie fires. By the time of Shirref's trip, Aux Sable timber had attracted a number of settlers, among them Salmon Rutherford, who had arrived from New York earlier that year. He had heard of plans to build a canal from Chicago to La Salle, and knew that its route would likely follow the old channel through Minooka Ridge. He built the tavern, and two years later, smitten with "canal fever," platted a town of sixty-three blocks along the river. For reasons known only to himself, he named it Dresden.

Seven years after Shirref made his journal entry, a British Army officer named Henry Francis Ainslie made the same stage trip. He was also moved by the view from Minooka Ridge, and rendered a watercolor of the Dresden settlement, now in the Chicago Historical Society. It shows the Stage Road winding into the distance toward the Aux Sable timber. But instead of the booming canal town envisioned by Rutherford, only two buildings in addition to the original tavern had been built. Rutherford's dream had suffered the same fate as other "paper town" developers along the line, despite his accurate prediction of the location of the canal route.

Its path is clear to me, marked by a line of trees, angling across the old Dresden townsite. Except for this, the scene (p. 26) is little changed from the day Colonel Ainslie painted it. Farmland has replaced the magnificent stand of oaks that gave respite to Shirref and his fellows. The eastern slope of the ridge is now a cemetery, partially overgrown with weeds. The silence is broken only by the wind and the crackling hum from heavy cables above my head, carrying electricity from the Dresden nuclear power plant across the river. Those aboriginal trails, that once linked tribes from the Upper Mississippi with those in the Illinois Valley, are now submerged below twenty feet of water impounded by the Dresden Lock and Dam.

Hansel Road, following the path of the Old Stage Road, still cuts across the townsite. It passes just south of an old farmhouse, formerly Rutherford's Tavern, before crossing the canal. The farmhouse is now owned by a Mr. Dollinger, who is with me on the ridge while I set up my camera. Earlier today, we had walked west along the canal towpath for a way, then back to his barn (plate 32), which he said was one of the "state barns," built at fifteen-mile intervals between locks for canal mules and horses. Inside, he showed me the massive wooden peg and tongue-and-groove joinings to prove its age.

Walking back to his house, we crossed his field, freshly planted in clover. He said that he raised three sons here, and for the last fifteen years, since the last left, he has run the farm alone, "plowing up," he said, "the entire sixty-three blocks of downtown Dresden."

Standing next to me now, he is looking down at his farm and remembering how Hansel Road "used to come right across this ridge, through a grove of big trees," just as it is shown in Ainslie's watercolor.

Marquette

We left behind us the waters that flowed toward Quebec and entered those that would thenceforward take us to strange lands.
—Père Marquette, 1673

During the demolition of an old house in Montreal in 1896, a cracked and deteriorated portrait of a young man, painted in oil on a wooden board, was discovered among the rubble. The eyes are large and contemplative, set beneath a high, smooth forehead. The nose is slightly aquiline. Although the lower part of the painting is blotched with age, encircling the neck the white collar of the cleric is unmistakable. On the back of the painting is carved the signature of the artist, "R. Roos, 1669," and the name "Marquette." Nothing more is known about the painting.

Since the beginning of French colonization of the New World, the Jesuits had followed the explorers and traders as they penetrated farther and farther into the wilderness. By 1632, a chain of missions had been established from Quebec to the Great Lakes, offering spiritual sustenance to the French and Christianity to the Indians. One of the most remote of these outposts was the mission at Sault Ste. Marie.

In 1666, Père Jacques Marquette, at the age of twenty-nine, arrived at Sault Ste. Marie, eager to begin the missionary duty for which he had prepared himself rigorously during the last twelve years in France. As a young novitiate he had shown an aptitude for language and a congenial disposition. He had no doubt read the *Relations,* diaries and letters from missionaries in the field, published annually in Paris by the Jesuits. Inspired by these accounts, Marquette had developed a strong desire to bring his faith to the New World. By the time he was ready for his first mission, his

Cross marking Marquette's winter stay in Chicago

inherent traits had been molded and guided by the Jesuit training toward his destiny among the Indians of New France.

But interspersed among the reports of the performance of pious duty and mundane observations on the character of the climate and soil, the *Relations* also contained stark accounts of torture and death suffered by Frenchmen at the hands of "savages." The Indians had an understandable hostility to outsiders, and their response to contact ranged from contemptuous indifference to extreme hatred. Because of their discipline and training in dealing with the Indians, it was customary for a Jesuit priest to accompany every exploratory expedition. In the 1673 volume of the *Relations,* this entry is found: "[Marquette] has both tact and prudence, which are the chief characteristics required for the success of a voyage as dangerous as it is difficult. He has the courage to dread nothing where everything is to be feared."

The voyage referred to was an expedition to discover the mouth of the Mississippi River. On being chosen as the spiritual complement to this mission led by Louis Joliet, Marquette wrote in his journal: "I found myself under the blessed necessity of exposing my life for this long cherished cause. . . . We were ready to do and suffer everything for so glorious an undertaking."[1]

And so, in the spring of 1673, with five companions in two birch-bark canoes, the pair paddled from Mackinac, across the northern waters of Lake Michigan, and followed the shore south to Green Bay. They descended the Mississippi as far as the mouth of the Arkansas River, where they were convinced by the local tribes that the river did indeed empty into the Gulf of Mexico, but that if they continued they would encounter hostile Indians or Spaniards. They considered their mission complete and turned northward, returning by way of the Illinois River, which they had heard offered a shorter route to Lake Michigan.

Marquette's is the first written record we have describing the Illinois Valley. In his journal he wrote: "We have seen nothing like this river that we enter, as regards its fertility of soil, its prairies and woods; its cattle, elk, deer, wildcats, bustards, swans, parroquets,

[1]Reuben Gold Thwaites, *Father Marquette* (New York: D. Appleton & Company, 1902), p. 137.

and even beaver. There are many small lakes and rivers. That on which we sailed is wide, deep and still, for 65 leagues."[2]

Seventeen hundred years before Marquette wrote these words, the glacial outwash from Lake Chicago down the valley had recently subsided, leaving as its legacy the Illinois River. By then, the natural abundance he observed had drawn Woodland period Indians to the valley, and occupation had begun at the rapids near a 140-foot limestone prominence Marquette called "the Rock." Upon reaching this point in the river, he made the following entry in his journal: "We found a village of the Illinois called Kaskaskia, consisting of 74 cabins. They received us well, and obliged me to promise that I would return to instruct them. One of the chiefs of the nation, with his young men, escorted us to the lake of the Illinois."[3] He then records the "portage of half a league" to the lake shown him by his Indian guides, the first historical reference to the Chicago Portage.

On their return to Green Bay in September, their exploratory mission was complete and Joliet left for Montreal. But Marquette, unable to quell his missionary zeal, remained to prepare for an ill-advised winter return to Kaskaskia. As the southern lake breezes of late October succumbed to the stormy portents of November, he paddled south along the shore, and in early December entered the Chicago River, heading for the newly discovered portage.

But he had traveled only a short distance up the river when he found his way blocked by ice, and with the help of his two boatmen, built a log hut. Here they settled in to wait for the spring thaw, living on dried meat and Indian corn. Indians from nearby tribes, hearing of Marquette's return, visited him during the winter. Near his hut they built a small altar over which was raised a wooden cross, similar, perhaps, to the one shown in the photograph on page 32, which was raised in remembrance of Marquette's winter there. It stands aside Damen Avenue, near the Stevenson Expressway, rising incongruously above the industrial milieu of Chicago's southwest side.

As cold, white drifts swirled outside the hut, Marquette's simmering spiritual ardor fought the fever that seized his body. Finally,

[2]H. W. Beckwith, ed., *Collections of the Illinois State Historical Society*, vol. 1 (Springfield: The H. W. Rokker Company, 1903), p. 40.
[3]Beckwith, *Collections of the Illinois State Historical Society*, p. 40.

one night in late March, cracks of melting ice split the night air and by morning they were up to their knees in icy mud and meltwater.

Marquette summed up his miserable winter at Chicago like this: "The blessed Virgin Immaculate has taken such care of us during our wintering that we have not lacked provisions, and still have left a large sack of corn and some fat. We also lived very pleasantly for my illness did not prevent my saying holy mass every day. We were unable to keep Lent except on Fridays and Saturdays."[4]

The monument shown in plate 36 stands on the grounds of St. Mary's Catholic Church in Utica. Marquette is in profile, facing east toward the site of Kaskaskia, a short distance up the Illinois River. Upon his return there in the spring after his Chicago winter, Marquette was welcomed as an "angel from heaven," and he immediately established a mission, naming it The Immaculate Conception. On April 14, 1675, he said his first mass there, the event memorialized by this granite relief.

Shortly thereafter, he said his last, for the illness contracted at Chicago worsened, and he was no longer able to perform the duty that had so consumed him. His final days were spent retracing the portage route to Lake Michigan. Returning to St. Ignace by taking the southern lake crossing and going up the eastern shore, he died near the present site of Ludington, Michigan, lying on the bare ground. His companions, honoring his wishes, erected a wooden cross over his grave.

It is possible that the young cleric who posed for R. Roos in 1669 was not the same as the one painted by the words of historical documents. Whoever the real Marquette, the authenticity of his sincerity and commitment to his calling has never been questioned. He was the embodiment of the best of the Jesuit philosophy, and his performance in the field was a model for Jesuit relations with the Indians for the next hundred years.

[4]Reuben Gold Thwaites, ed., *Travels and Explorations of the Jesuit Missionaries in New France, 1610–1791*, vol. 59 (Cleveland: The Burrows Brothers Company, 1900), p. 181.

Saganashkee Slough, south of Mount Forest Island. These swampy lowlands are remnants of the glacial outwash channel through the Valparaiso Moraine from ancient Lake Chicago.

Mount Forest Island

A canal . . . would afford facilities commensurate with the great
thoroughfares it would connect.
                                        —*Chicago Democrat*, 10 December 1834

Around the southern edge of Lake Michigan, contour maps reveal a series of low, crescent-shaped uplands rippling inland from the shore, stretching for two hundred miles south across the flat plains of Illinois. These are terminal moraines, formed around the margins of ice tongues as the various lobes of the Wisconsin glacier retreated northward at the end of the Pleistocene epoch.

The moraine nearest the lake, outlining the ice fringe before its final withdrawal across the basin, is called the Valparaiso moraine. The size and shape of Cape Cod, it arches ten to forty miles inland, cradling the southwest rim of the lake shore, from the Wisconsin border to the dunes of northwestern Indiana. Fifteen thousand years ago, the great white cusp of the Lake Michigan lobe stagnated, forming this moraine around its melting edge. For more than two hundred years, the ice flowing from the north just balanced the melting loss; the moving ice was like a continental conveyer belt, dumping tons of entrained rubble and granite from as far away as the Canadian Shield.

As the glacier melted back, its water was trapped in the basin between this moraine and the ice barrier to the north. The lake that was formed, which was much larger than the present Lake Michigan, is referred to by geologists as glacial Lake Chicago, one of several bodies of meltwater that spread across the Great Lakes basins at various times during the Pleistocene. Drainage to the Atlantic through the St. Lawrence was blocked by the ice, so the rising water of Lake Chicago eventually found an outlet to the southwest through two small depressions in the Valparaiso moraine. The volume of water being released by the glacier was tremendous, and the flow became a torrent, easily cutting through the soft silt of the moraine.

The two outlets across the top of the moraine were separated by about a mile of upland, and their channels merged two miles from their exit points from the lake. Between these channels was a wedge-shaped island, its southwestern tip formed at the V by the merger of the two channels. On maps representing the Pleistocene topography, the island looks like a plug lifted slightly from the Lake Chicago drainpipe.

This plug of land is now called Mount Forest Island, a name that incorporates its past and present aspect, and is about twelve miles southwest of Chicago's Loop. Most of the upland surface is a forest preserve, and its glacial origin is evident in the rolling terrain and rounded depressions of more than a dozen small lakes.

Dug in the bed of the northernmost of the two outlet channels, bordering Mount Forest Island, is the I&M Canal. During the canal's construction, there was a small community of workers near the point of merger of the two former channels, and a church, St. James Sag (plate 33) was built on the overlooking hill. The headstones in its cemetery (plate 34) are the only monuments to the many Irish workers who lived there and in other towns along the canal, who shoveled sludge and mud for a dollar a day in that swampy ditch, infested with mosquitos and festering with malaria. Those who survived got a piece of land at a bargain; those who did not got a much smaller plot here or in other cemeteries along the route.

I have been photographing in the cemetery, and I begin walking down the steep slope toward the intersection of Archer Avenue and Calumet Sag Road. Archer Avenue parallels the canal and was built as an access road during its construction. Calumet Sag Road follows the channel cut by the southern branch of the Lake Chicago Outlet. They intersect at the southwestern tip of the wedge where the two outwash channels met.

Three thousand years ago, the roar from the rush of the merging rivers would have been deafening. Now, the guttural clatter of diesel trucks loaded with gravel deposited by that flow drowns out the crisp rustle of my feet in the layer of October leaves. To the southwest, through the white industrial haze, I can see the broad valley carved out by the combined energy of these two rivers. Through this valley for five thousand years flowed the glacial outwash, its downstream inundations, erosions, and depositions creating the rich landscape of the upper Illinois valley that was so attractive to the aboriginal tribes and the early French traders and explorers.

Crossing the intersection at the foot of the hill, I follow Calumet Sag Road as it leaves the old south channel, loses its geographical context and becomes Robert Kingery Road, bridging across the northern valley. Beneath the bridge run the I&M Canal and two other slivers of water, bundled between two railroad tracks. The northernmost waterway is the Des Plaines River, natural heir to the old channel. It rises to the northeast, just west of the Lake Michigan basin, and flows to the southwest. About thirty-five miles downstream, it is joined by the Kankakee River, itself tracing another glacial sluiceway from the Lake Erie basin, and together they form the Illinois River. During the 170 years following its discovery by Marquette and Joliet in 1673, this waterway was the route of traders, missionaries, and explorers traveling between the Chicago Portage and the interior valley settlements. One of these travelers was Father Jean Francois Buisson de St. Cosme, sent by the Bishop of Canada to establish missions in the Southwest. In a letter to the Bishop in 1699, St. Cosme wrote of the Des Plaines: "The banks of this river are very agreeable; they consist of prairies bounded by small hills and very fine thickets; there are a number of deer in them and along the river are great quantities of game of all kinds."[1]

Now, as I look down from the bridge, those agreeable banks that once bordered the river in its free meanders across the channel run as straight as plowed furrows, and along the river are great quantities of industrial detritus of all kinds.

Across from the river, following the southern contour of the old channel, is the I&M Canal, barely visible through the foliage. This reach of the canal, between the Chicago River and Lockport, was originally at summit level, eight feet above Lake Michigan. But as the population of Chicago grew, so did the volume of its effluent, and the city realized that its recurring epidemics of typhoid were caused by dumping raw sewage into the Lake Michigan water supply. So in

---

[1]Paul M. Angle, ed., *Prairie State: Impressions of Illinois, 1673–1967, by Travellers and Other Observers* (Chicago: The University of Chicago Press, 1968), p. 31.

1871, the previously abandoned "deep cut" plan was implemented, and the bottom of the canal was dredged to lake level, causing water to flow directly from the Chicago River down the canal to the Illinois River, in a Lilliputian reinstitution of the glacial torrent that had originally carved the valley. The belief that free-flowing water would naturally cleanse itself allayed the fears of those downstream, and the city watched as gravity flushed its sewage problem far downstream.

Curving southwest from the bridge, between the channelized Des Plaines River and the slender, overgrown prism of the I&M Canal, is a much wider waterway—the Sanitary and Ship Canal. From around the curve, about a half mile away, I see three mountains of gravel, approaching single file. Beyond, a smudge of black smoke is rising, and soon a tug comes into view. A few minutes later, the shadow of the bridge bends across the conical peaks as the barge slowly emerges from beneath, and I can feel the bridge vibrating in response to the low rumble of the straining diesels.

The continued expansion of Chicago rendered the capacity of the deepened I&M Canal inadequate, both as a sewage conduit and for bulk freight, passenger service having ceased long before in favor of the railroads. So in 1892 construction began on the Sanitary and Ship Canal, the largest of the three waterways under the bridge, and the only one navigable by commercial vessels. This reach between Chicago and Lockport was opened in 1900, its dual purpose so succinctly summed up in its name, and it effectively replaced the corresponding section of the I&M Canal, hastening the decline in its use. In 1933, the Sanitary and Ship Canal became part of the Illinois Waterway, a deep-water passage between the Great Lakes and the Gulf of Mexico, and the eighty-five-year service of the I&M Canal ended with its unceremonious closure.

The barge is now about a mile upstream, moving slowly toward Chicago. A trestle bridge of angled steel has opened, poised like a giant black mantis above the passing mounds of gravel. The tracks of the Atchison, Topeka, and Santa Fe Railroad cross the trestle, pass under the bridge beneath me, and head southwest between the rusting clutter of Jerry's Valley Auto Parts and the towpath of the I&M Canal. In 1854, six years after the canal was completed, engines of the Rock Island began steaming along this same bed, past canal mules pulling packets full of passengers. These "fast" packets carried passengers at six miles per hour between Chicago and La Salle, where steamboat connections for the Illinois River were made. At the time the canal opened, the serenity of travel along its route was a novel alternative to the stagecoaches bumping along the dusty trails during dry seasons and mired in mud otherwise. In 1847, J. H. Buckingham, son of the publisher of the *Boston Courier,* traveled by stagecoach from Chicago to Peru, and described his ride as "uncomfortable as any enemy, if we had one, could desire. We made progress at the rate of less than three miles per hour; the weather was intensely hot, and not a breath of air was stirring; the horse and carriage raised any quantity of dust, which, of course, rose only high enough to fill the carriage; and we were nine inside passengers."[2]

But the whistle of the train was the knell of the canal. Within a few months, its passenger service was usurped by the railroads, leaving as its only function the transport of bulk freight. Much of that bulk was, ironically, material for the rails and ties of the tracks being constructed in its own right-of-way.

In places where the canal was dug through narrow geological constrictions, the railroad bed was laid less than a hundred feet away. Between Utica and La Salle, about seventy miles southwest of this bridge, the canal and tracks converge between the high northern bluffs and the swampy bottomlands of the Illinois River valley. Once, while photographing among the canyons eroded into the limestone of these bluffs, I left the towpath and walked some distance along the track. I was immediately struck by the change in the ambience from the shaded banks of the canal to the gleaming steel of the rails. I stooped and ran my finger across the mirrored surface of the track, and I reflected on the drastic shift in humanity's orientation toward the landscape that must have accompanied its transformation by the industrial revolution.

I looked down the tracks; they offered no place for the eye to rest, stretching away in linear homogeneity, remaining rigid even in bending. Spiked to ties uniformly spaced in no-nonsense monotony, the tracks seemed indifferent to the land, elevated on a bed of gravel, with less regard for the natural contours of the land than the canal, entrenched in its earthen prism. I considered the elemental simplicity of water moving by gravity, and boats moving by the muscles

[2]Angle, *Prairie State*, p. 244.

of harnessed beasts, and I understood how the fire-driven "iron horse" could have seemed alien and intrusive.

But intrusion into the wilderness was the order of the day in the nineteenth century, and in this respect the railroads demonstrated superiority. Two years after the Erie Canal opened in 1825, the first steam locomotive was built in this country. By 1836, when work began on the I&M Canal, there were 948 miles of railroad compared to more than 2,600 miles of canal. When the first canal boat went down the I&M, twelve years later, more than 4,000 additional miles of track had been laid and canal construction had almost ceased.

In fact, it could be argued that the development of northeastern Illinois would have been little different had the canal never been dug. By the early 1830s, there was sentiment among the more prescient politicians that the railroads were the mode of the future and that tracks, not a ditch, were needed.

The issue dominated the campaigns of 1834 for the General Assembly and the governorship. Those in favor of a railroad pointed out that a railroad would be cheaper to construct and maintain; it would have greater durability and would provide cheaper, faster transportation. They also noted that for four months of the year, even though the connecting waterways would remain open, the canal would be frozen.

Those favoring the canal appealed to fears of the unknown, referring to the "complications of machinery, and the consequent liability to accident." They accused the opposition of having their "imaginations held captive to the flying motion of a railroad car." They also argued that a railroad would be less harmonious with the landscape than a water route, disrupting the natural relationship between Lake Michigan and the Illinois River, that "a canal . . . would afford facilities commensurate with the great thoroughfares it would connect."[3]

The conservative sentiment won in the elections of 1834, but in 1854, only six years after the canal opened, the railroad bed for the Rock Island Line (plate 20) was laid, and trains began steaming through the canal right-of-way.

[3]*House Committee Reports*, No. 546, 23d Congress, 1st Session, p. 14. Walter A. Howe, *Documentary History of the Illinois and Michigan Canal* (Springfield, IL: Division of Waterways, State of Illinois, 1956), p. 25.

Thus the steam engine, a more effective vehicle in the American drive to exploit the interior, became the lasting symbol of the westward adventure; the canals, always an Old World graft on the New, withered.

Dry leaves are falling from the branches overhanging the stagnant water of the abandoned canal. They stick in the scum where they land, mottling the green surface with brown and gold. The railroad trestle has closed behind the barge; I head toward the other side of the bridge, where Kingery Road rises steeply to the crest of a bluff. The walkway between the road and the bridge railing is narrow, and I feel the air rush against my back as dust swirls at my feet when heavy trucks pass, building momentum for the climb. Once across the bridge, I move away from the road and follow a quieter path through the trees to the top of the ridge.

This is one of the highest of the rounded hills that the glacier engraved across the top of the Valparaiso moraine. Twelve thousand years ago, after the ice front had melted back across the basin, lake waves and wind formed a sandy beach on the eastern slope of the moraine, sixty feet above and twelve miles to the west of today's Oak Street Beach on Lake Michigan. Called the Glenwood stage by geologists, it is the highest of a series of decreasing lake levels recorded in the sands of beaches and dunes now buried beneath streets and buildings in elevations around the basin. Once while hiking in a forest preserve near here, I scooped up sand from beneath the topsoil and, as it sifted through my fingers, imagined looking out across that glacial lakescape. It is winter, and as far as I can see, the jagged edges of ice floes jostle against one another, rolling and cracking in the crystalline air above the surface of the lake. Water sloshes in the crevices between the ice, appearing as blue thunderbolts striking across the white expanse toward the horizon. In summer, the shore would be free of ice, but the air would be chilled and the lake would still be spotted with ice patches drifting slowly southward in the current. Farther out would be larger masses—miniature icebergs—calved from the melting face of the glacier still rimming the northern shore of the lake. If the air were clear, an island would be visible to the southeast, just this side of the horizon, with waves washing across the low sand spit extending from its northern tip.

If I were to follow Kingery Road to the south, back across the bridge and past its intersection with Archer Avenue, where it becomes Calumet Sag Road, and continue east down the old southern outwash channel for ten miles, I would pass the southern tip of this island. In deference to its former stature it was named Blue Island, but now it is just a bump in the flow of Chicago's street grid.

From the bluff, at eye level across the valley, is St. James Sag Church on Mount Forest Island, its spire rising among the headstones scattered down the surrounding slope. During the time of outflow from Lake Chicago, that slope was awash with glacial meltwater, and the view from this bluff would have been spectacular: a moving mass of water a hundred times greater than the flow over Niagara Falls, carrying chunks of ice the size of trucks. Downstream, it carved a valley a mile wide and three hundred feet deep through Ordovician limestone bedrock. Evidence of its enormous power can be seen in the eroded faces of bluffs a hundred miles south, and the volume of its flow measured by the massive depositions of gravel and sand along its bed. It pooled behind morainal dams forming huge reservoirs, then emptied, spilling in braided cascades through narrow sluiceways. It mingled with water from other melting lobes to the west flowing through the Mississippi Valley, and finally spread a layer of glacial silt from the north across the delta as it flowed into the Gulf of Mexico.

But now the valley is empty and still. Across the bridge, a single truck loaded with gravel emerges in a blossom of white dust from a quarry road, turning onto Kingery Road. As the truck grinds its gears up the slope toward me, the dust slowly disperses and rises, mingling with the white layer already suspended over the valley. The top of the cloud reaches almost to my eye level, masking the headstones on Mount Forest Island, across the valley, behind a veil of white translucence. A breeze is blowing from the northeast, and the cloud floats silently down the valley in ghostly semblance of that ancient Pleistocene outwash.

But I have a sense that this scene is also a portent, that this valley abides for the time when the ice, in response to some slight disturbance in the flow of earth's energy, stirs from its Greenland dormancy and reclaims the landscape that we now exploit as our own. By then, the resources bequeathed us by the last advance of the ice will have long since been spent, and the artifacts of our industry will be embedded in the layer of silt, sand, and gravel deposited by the next.

The City of Pekin

The frogs bellowed in the marshes all night, we were plagued with insects, and to make matters worse, the stupid boatman simply let the mules out to graze, throwing the reins over a stone, and then falling asleep and snoring loudly. At dawn, one of the passengers discovered we had been making no progress, leaped ashore, and gave the boatman a terrific beating.
— The poet Horace, describing his ride on a Roman canal boat, during the reign of Agrippa

During the 1860s and 1870s, as many as 228 boats operated on the I&M Canal. Before 1870, all were built as "tow" boats: designed to be drawn by horses or mules driven down the towpath (plate 37). Around 1870, steam-powered boats began service, and after 1880, all boats were built with steam engines.

Boat designs depended on the purpose of the boat; the two basic types being the passenger packet and the freight boat. Packets were sixty to eighty feet long and ten to fifteen feet wide. The passenger accommodations of one of them are described in this account by a British army officer in 1850:

On Saturday evening, the 12th of October, about 5 P.M., I embarked on board the canal boat, the "Queen of the Prairies," bound for La Salle, a town situated southwest of Chicago, about 100 miles distant, and at the head of the navigable portion of the Illinois River. The cabin of this canal boat was about 50 feet in length, 9 feet wide, and 7 feet high. We numbered about ninety passengers within this confined space, in which we were to sleep, eat, and live; the nominal duration of our passage was twenty-four hours, but it eventually proved to be twenty-five; our baggage was secure on the roof of the boat, and covered with

45

Keel of the *City of Pekin* in the dry canal bed, Channahon. *Middle Division, Mile 44, El. 518 ft. (62 ft. below lake level)*

canvas, to screen it from the effects of the weather. A sort of divan surrounded the cabin, the portion appropriated to the ladies being screened off during the night with a curtain.[1]

After the 1850s, when rail service began between Chicago and La Salle, passenger packets were no longer used and canal revenue was derived solely from bulk freight.

Freight boats were from 90 to 107 feet long and could carry up to a hundred tons. They were of two basic designs: the grain boats with two covered holds for carrying corn or wheat, and the stone boats with an open deck for transporting stone from quarries near the line.

Steamboats were based on the design of the grain boats, but were modified to accommodate a pilot house, twin steam engines, and the propulsion screws. During the 1870s, grain boats were sometimes converted to steamboats.

The *City of Henry,* built in Chicago in 1875, was a ninety-nine-foot steamboat. Its width was seventeen feet, with a capacity of ninety-five tons of grain. Joseph W. Foster, the captain, was born in a canal boat between Seneca and Morris, a two- or three-generation "canaller" family not being unusual. For nineteen years, the *City of Henry* was part of a fleet at Lockport that operated on the canal and between ports on the Illinois River.

Foster's daughter, Helen, grew up on the *City of Henry* and still remembers how she used to "help" him steer the boat standing on a box in the pilot house. In vivid detail from indelible impressions of childhood she describes the interior of the cabin:

> The fore cabin was the sleeping quarters of the deck hands. The walls were tongue and groove lumber painted creme colored. There was a board floor with a rag rug. As you stepped into the cabin there was a step down, a bunk bed on either side, windows were sliding ones with green shades. Under the windows at the back was a shelf with a wash basin, a small mirror on the wall, a couple of hooks for hanging the "go to town clothes." A towel hung on the door. A lantern was used for lighting, and

[1]Paul M. Angle, ed., *Prairie State: Impressions of Illinois, 1673–1967, by Travellers and Other Observers* (Chicago: The University of Chicago Press, 1968), p. 255.

stored on the shelf. The sheets and pillow cases were dark blue with small white figures (calico) and dark blankets. In front of the cabin stood a huge ice box and a large water tank. The tank was filled before leaving Pekin as the water in southern Illinois might be contaminated. There was a lot of malaria at the time.

The main cabin or captain's quarters had three rooms. The front half was a dining room and kitchen. The back was divided in half with bunk beds on either side. Between the two bedrooms was a door, and the doors from the dining room-kitchen had curtains made of drapery material. Not much privacy, but this was mostly a family affair.[2]

By the 1890s, canal commerce was ebbing on the flow of Chicago sewage, and in 1894, the *City of Henry* was moved from Lockport to Henry, on the Illinois River. There it was rebuilt for operation on the river. Seventeen years later, it was modified again, but by this time the I&M trade was so insignificant that the pilot house was raised to fifteen feet, making it too high to navigate under the bridges of the canal. After this rebuilding, the name of the boat was changed to the *City of Pekin* and for the next thirty years it operated exclusively as a river boat.

By the 1930s, the *City of Pekin*, like the canal, had become a relic and was rotting in the shallows of the river. After the canal was formally closed in 1933, the state realized that the *City of Pekin* was the only remaining boat of the entire canal fleet, and it was hauled from the river and tied to the canal bank at Channahon. In 1937, a survey was conducted of its condition in preparation for restoring it as an attraction in the planned Illinois and Michigan Canal Parkway. The homey interior of Helen Foster's reminiscences bears little resemblence to the boat described in the survey report:

The *City of Pekin* at the time it was surveyed, had its stern cut off at the center of the third hatch. . . . The workmanship on this ship was of the poorest quality we have seen. The *City of Pekin* did not have a keel. The planks were nailed to the frames and a 3″ × 11½″ white pine board was nailed to the frames as a

[2]Helen Foster Poole to John Lamb, December 5, 1978, Illinois Canal Society Files, Lewis University, Romeoville, Illinois.

keelson. The stanchions were toenailed into the keelson instead of mortise and tenon.[3]

Four years after the survey, and still unrestored, the *City of Pekin* burned to the waterline. The photograph on page 46 was taken a hundred yards east of Lock 7 at Channahon and shows the remains of Helen's boat, including the white pine board mentioned in the survey, embedded in the dry canal bottom.

[3]City of Pekin Report, Works Progress Administration, Survey 14–19, Historic American Merchant Marine Survey. Chicago Project 64–6, Watercraft Collection, Smithsonian Institution, Washington, D.C., June 11, 1937.

Outcropping of limestone and overlying Pennsylvanian coal, Buffalo
Rock

Buffalo Rock

There is nothing inorganic. . . . The earth is not a fragment of dead history, stratum upon stratum, like the leaves of a book, to be studied by geologists and antiquaries chiefly, but living poetry, like the leaves of a tree, which precede flowers and fruit; not a fossil earth but a living earth.
                                        —Henry David Thoreau, 1854

The grunting laborers digging the canal probably gave little thought to the yellow chunks they were heaving up from the bottom of the prism. That interest would come later, from those who noted the fortuitous discovery of valuable minerals coincident with the creation of the means of their transportation.

Beyond its immediate practical purpose, the canal was a hundred-mile excavation through a wonderfully rich and complex geology. At one place or another along its path the workers dug through beds of outwash gravel and alluvium from Lake Chicago, layers of glacial till, deposits of coal and sandstone, and lenses of limestone, each shovelful the distillation of sixty thousand years of geological history.

But it was the potential wealth, not Thoreau's "living poetry," of that "stratum upon stratum" that attracted the nineteenth-century entrepreneurs. Even before the canal was completed, these materials were being mined for construction of its locks, and the character of the corridor would come to be defined by these underlying strata, each mineral being extracted for its respective industry.

North of Utica, beneath a foot or two of soil and glacial silt, the canal workers dug into white sandstone, almost pure quartz, laid down by the advance of Ordovician seas, blown into dunes by winds, covered and preserved so well that in some places the ripples

51

made by ocean waves four hundred million years ago were still visible. It became known as St. Peter sandstone, and from it was derived the best glassmaking sand in the world.

After the seas receded, plants growing on the marshy surface formed the Pennsylvanian coal measures that spread from here southward. A two-foot band, the northern tip of the measures, is shown resting on a layer of St. Peter sandstone in a road cut at Buffalo Rock (p. 50). Above the coal can be seen another layer of sand, deposited much later by the Kankakee torrent, in one of the meltwater surges released from glaciers in the Great Lakes basin. The sand was covered in turn by the topsoil, a mixture of loess and the organic remains of plants and roots formed on the top of Buffalo Rock since the torrent subsided fifteen thousand years ago.

Beginning in 1934, forty million years of coal formation, represented by the strata shown here, was stripped from the top of Buffalo Rock within just eight years. The soil still supports very little vegetation, due to the acidity of the strip mining spoils, and will probably remain barren for the lifetime of most people reading this book (plate 38).

Ninety feet below the bottom layer of sandstone in the photograph runs a vein of Shakopee dolomite that bulges up near Utica and was the basis of the town's early cement works. South of Utica, at Split Rock, it plunges a thousand feet below the surface, the leading edge of a wave moving through the earth reverberating from distant continental upheavals lifting the Allegheny Mountains.

"Irish Rebellion"

*I beheld with sorrow one wide waste of putrefying vegetation,
the entire green countryside appearing scorched, as if a fire had
passed over.*
—A priest traveling from Cork to Dublin, Ireland, in July, 1846

The potato famine in Ireland between 1847 and 1851 dramatized in a terrible way the problems that beset that country in the mid-nineteenth century. During those years, a million people died and another million immigrated to America. When the blight struck, two-thirds of the Irish population were tenant farmers tilling plots of land less than five acres, on which they had to support their large families. This situation was a result of the practices of the absentee landlords, mostly British, who found it profitable to subdivide the farms into smaller and smaller parcels. To make the most productive use of these small plots, the farmers had begun to rely solely on the potato for sustenance, since its yield per acre in nourishment far exceeded any other crop.

By the early nineteenth century, the exploitation of the tenant farmers by their landlords, the establishment of Protestantism as the official church, and the suppression of the native Irish language had combined to make life intolerable for many Catholics. At the same time, they were receiving letters from friends and relatives in America, describing the vastness of the frontier, the freedom from oppression, and, above all, the promise of property ownership.

In contrast to the oppression in Ireland, the Americans were engaged in a frenzy of internal improvements, advancing into the interior with the technology and implements of the Industrial Revolution. One of the first problems addressed was transportation, both among East Coast towns and over the Allegheny Mountains to the

Dry canal bed, between Utica and La Salle, near the site of the final confrontation of the "Irish Rebellion." *Western Division, Mile 92, El. 465 ft. (115 ft. below lake level)*

Mississippi drainage basin. Linking natural waterways by canals was a proven technique, and by 1840 all but four of the states east of the Mississippi had at least one in operation.

By a historical coincidence, the need for labor in America for these public works occurred just as thousands were being forced to emigrate from Ireland. In 1820, advertisements for workers for the Chesapeake and Ohio Canal were placed in Irish newspapers, promising food, liquor, and wages. The response was a flood of laborers, most willing to work for low pay under conditions shunned by other groups. A substantial portion of the labor for canal construction throughout the country was Irish: five thousand worked on the Erie Canal and nearly two thousand on the Wabash-Erie Canal in Indiana. When work began on the I&M, Irish laborers were recruited in Canada and in the east, and by 1838 there were hundreds living in shanty towns along the line. Despite the rosy picture that the advertisements painted, the working conditions on the I&M were deplorable: the pay was a dollar for a sixteen-hour workday, and outbreaks of cholera and other diseases claimed hundreds. A visitor to the construction sites in 1839 wrote: "Laboring from day to day in low lands and stagnant water, human life has proved to be very short. Out of 1500 laboring men employed on the canal, 1000 died during this past year of over-exertion and the diseases incident to the climate, fever and ague and bilious weather."[1]

Often workers were cheated by unscrupulous contractors, and more than once they were paid in virtually useless scrip. During the summer, temperatures rose to 110 degrees and in the lowlands the crew were often engulfed by swarms of mosquitos, against which they had few defenses.

Despite the sorry working conditions, there was only one two-week strike during the entire twelve-year project, and only one serious occurrence of violence. The credit for this relatively harmonious atmosphere belongs to William Gooding, the chief engineer, whose sense of compassion for the workers was as strong as his engineering skill.

In early 1838, a dispute broke out in the labor camps near Marseilles between two factions, Catholic Corkonians and Protes-

[1]Catherine Tobin, "The Lowly Muscular Diggers: Irish Canal Workers in the Nineteenth Century" (Ph.D. diss., Notre Dame, 1987), p. 129.

tant Fardowners. The immediate issue was the belief among the Corkonians that Fardowners, or "Leinster men," were being favored in getting canal jobs, there being several Fardowners among the contractors.

The Corkonians battered the Fardowners in their first encounter, encouraging them to more violence, and they rampaged down the line toward Peru, attacking Fardowners on sight. A priest at La Salle witnessed part of the incident and wrote to his bishop:

> Yesterday afternoon at five about two hundred Irishmen passed through LaSalle armed with guns and sharp sticks. Without any reason they went down to Peru insulting the people of the adverse province. Many were beaten so badly that they were bleeding heavily. At night they camped about a mile away from our house, almost all of them under the influence of liquor. . . . They were resolved to burn all the houses along the Line that belong to people of the hated province. . . . I assure you that I never heard anything like this: now I know how national passion can carry people to these excesses.[2]

For three days the Corkonians rioted up and down the line, pursued by the sheriff's posse, until the final confrontation just east of Buffalo Rock, near where the photograph on page 54 was taken. The posse, unable to handle the hostility and defiance any other way, finally fired into the crowd, then charged them on their horses. The rioters scattered; some were pursued on foot toward Buffalo Rock and others jumped in the river and were shot while swimming away.

Ten to fifteen Corkonians were killed, many were injured, and sixty were captured and jailed in Ottawa.

[2]Tobin, "The Lowly Muscular Diggers," p. 185.

The Western Division

To really come to an understanding of a specific American geography requires not only time but a kind of local expertise, an intimacy with place few of us ever develop.
—Barry Lopez, 1989

During my photographic trips along the canal, I was drawn many times to the western stretch of the old route between Ottawa and the terminus at La Salle. The tangled ruggedness of the undeveloped terrain, the geological and floral diversity, and the evidences of industry offered an endless source of material for my camera and my thoughts. Nowhere else in the corridor is the intertwining of human history, geography, and geology so well expressed as along this eighteen-mile section.

The northern bluffs of the valley shadow the canal in its fifty-one-foot drop through five locks from the aqueduct over the Fox River to the junction with the Illinois River at La Salle. Running beneath the bed of the canal is a layer of 480-million-year-old sedimentary bedrock, known geologically as Shakopee dolomite. It inclines gradually upward to the west and intersects the canal prism near Utica. In 1837, while this section of the canal was being excavated, the shovels of the canal workers struck this strata, and within a year it was being mined to produce cement for the locks and dams.

The first lock west of Ottawa is Lock 11, located to take advantage of an ancient fall of water in the floor of the outlet river. Just south of the lock, a sand pit was dug in 1900, mining the pure silica sand from the St. Peter sandstone. Since then, more than a hundred million tons of sand have been removed from this and other quarries along the canal. A mile and a half west is Lock 12 (p. 58). A

Lock 12, west of Ottawa. *Western Division, Mile 84, El. 481 ft. (99 ft. below lake level)*

few yards east of this lock the canal passes the mouth of Falls Canyon, one of a half dozen ravines cut deeply through limestone bluffs by streams emptying into the alluvial floodplain of the river valley. From 1887 to 1953, the mouth of Falls Canyon was the site of a company town called Twin Bluffs, manufacturing brick and drain tile from the shale and clay mined in the bluffs nearby.

Five thousand years ago, the surface of the outlet river from Lake Chicago flowed sixty feet above this section of canal towpath. During spring flooding, a cutoff developed to the north and the river looped out and back in a small meander around a bedrock plug in its bed. For two thousand years, the river eroded the soft sandstone around this chunk of rock until, when the flow finally stopped, a 150-foot-high platform, now called Buffalo Rock, was left protruding from the river bed.

West of Lock 12 the canal was dug through that floodwater cutoff in the old riverbed between Buffalo Rock and the northern bluff. The rock was part of the federal land grant for the canal, and the first settlers found the remains of structures probably dating from the French era of activity in the valley. There had been at least two forts built on Buffalo Rock: one in 1687 to protect the Illinois tribes from the Iroquois, and another seventy years later during the French and Indian War, a final attempt to maintain a French stronghold in the valley.

Looking downriver from the top of Buffalo Rock, along the northern shore of the river, can be seen the site of Kaskaskia, the central village of the Illinois tribes in the seventeenth century. The written history of the valley began with Marquette's description of this "great village," and it is mentioned repeatedly by subsequent travelers. In 1677, Father Claude Allouez observed 351 lodges. A member of La Salle's 1680 expedition to the mouth of the Mississippi River, Friar Membré, wrote that it contained "seven or eight thousand souls."[1]

[1]H. W. Beckwith, ed., *Collections of the Illinois State Historical Society*, vol. 1 (Springfield: The H.W. Rokker Co., 1903), p. 40. Reuben Gold Thwaites, ed., *Travels and Explorations of the Jesuit Missionaries in New France, 1610–1791*, vol. 59 (Cleveland: The Burrows Brothers Company, 1900), p. 181. Francis Parkman, *La Salle and the Discovery of the Great West* (Williamstown, MA: Corner House Publishers, 1980), p. 169.

But by 1700, because of continuing attacks by the Iroquois, the Illinois had abandoned Kaskaskia and moved downriver, and for 150 years the exact location of the village was not known. In the 1860s, Francis Parkman retraced La Salle's journey down the Illinois and concluded that the landscape described in old French journals coincided with his own observations of the topography. In *La Salle and the Discovery of the Great West* he writes:

> Go to the banks of the Illinois where it flows by the Village of Utica, and stand on the meadow that borders it on the north. In front glides the river, a musket-shot in width; and from the farther bank rises, with gradual slope, a range of wooded hills that hide from sight the vast prairie behind them. A mile or more on your left these gentle acclivities end abruptly in the lofty front of the great cliff, called by the French the Rock of St. Louis [Starved Rock], looking boldly out from the forests that environ it.[2]

Farmers across the river from the rock showed Parkman some Indian artifacts from the floodplain turned up by their plows, convincing him that the rapids near Utica were the ones that had attracted the Indians to Kaskaskia. His conclusion was confirmed by archaeological work in the twentieth century.

The rapids, now submerged beneath the backwaters of Starved Rock Dam, marked a fall line in the Illinois River bed. Upstream the river flows through ancient bedrock channels cut through solid rock; downstream it spreads into an alluvial plain, navigable to the Mississippi River. This line was the upriver limit of navigation, and Utica, established in the early 1800s, became a transfer point for trade goods between riverboats from St. Louis and wagons from Chicago.

In the early 1830s, as various canal routes were being considered, the prospects for Utica remaining a center of trade were good, since one of the plans called for the canal to join the river there. However, political maneuverings led to the terminus being located at La Salle, six miles to the west, and the canal finally passed more than three miles north of Utica.

The canal immediately replaced the overland trade route, elim-

[2]Parkman, *La Salle and the Discovery of the Great West*, pp. 220–21.

inating Utica's position as a trade center. But the town's transition had already begun: in 1838, a hydraulic cement plant—the first in Illinois—was in operation based on the vein of limestone struck in the canal excavation the year before. Other plants followed, and Utica was able to carve an economic niche as a supplier of raw materials and products extracted from the surrounding rich deposits of minerals. In the early 1850s, the town shifted north to the canal, and the old site on the river was abandoned.

Of all the towns along the corridor, none has retained its nineteenth-century ambience as has Utica. It is still a quarry town, mining the same St. Peter sandstone and dolomite used for the I&M Canal locks. For a hundred years its population has remained a stable thousand, spreading little beyond the natural boundaries of the northern bluffs and the floodplain. Scattered about the surrounding woods and up in the canyons are the relics of early mining and quarrying enterprises. Like forsaken shrines, they rise from dense entanglements, stone testimony to the determination of the settlers in wresting what wealth they could from these veins before moving on, and also to the countervailing persistence of nature.

Though Utica is set in an unusually rich milieu of history and geology, it has remained unselfconscious and refreshingly free of tourist trappings. The surrounding ruins, including the canal locks themselves, have been preserved through neglect rather than conscious restoration; I have been startled by stumbling upon stone foundations shrouded in the underbrush. From their touch the reality of those times seems mysteriously drawn forth, their images more vivid than those of place mat maps and served-up simplifications of history.

Downriver from Utica, the canal cut has exposed the Shakopee vein: the oldest surface rock in Illinois. It can be seen in intermittent outcroppings tilting upward, and at Pecumsaugan Canyon, a mile west, it is forty feet above the canal towpath. I hiked a quarter mile up the canyon, following stones in the creek shallows to avoid the dense foliage on either side. Resting for a moment, I sensed a chill from above, air flowing from the mouth of an abandoned mine tunneled deep into the Shakopee vein. At my feet, nestled below the openings, was a patch of mountain holly, a floral remnant of the Pleistocene, living in the microspheric refuge of the mineshaft airflow.

On the other side of the creek I encountered the abandoned kilns of the Blackball Mines (plates 41 and 42). The Shakopee was known locally as the Blackball Vein and was mined by the Utica Cement Company in the 1870s. In these kilns the dolomite was converted into quicklime. Chunks were dumped into the top and heated, a process called calcining, which removed the carbon dioxide leaving rocky clinkers of calcium oxide. After calcining, the clinkers were removed from the arched openings. When ground to powder, they produced natural cement, also called hydraulic because it would harden under water, and for that reason was suitable as mortar for the locks and dams of the canal. There were four kilns here, each forty-five feet high with a brick superstructure resting on the stone base that remains.

It is apparent from plate 42 that the inside brick linings of the arches were replaced after an earlier period of abandonment. It is unlikely, however, that this mine was in operation much later than the turn of the century, since after that Portland cement, a much superior product than natural cement, became widely available.

During the years when canal boats were being loaded with clinkers, this was a raucous company town, complete with its own blacksmith shop, tavern, and school. But now an almost impenetrable wildness prevails, and nothing remains but the empty shafts that have become hibernacula for bats, and these spent kilns, disintegrating in the twisted foliage.

From Pecumsaugan Canyon, that great two-hundred-foot slab of Ordovician coral, the Shakopee, still slopes up to the west. But a mile away it has buckled and is tilted back down—geologically the La Salle Anticline—and passes through Split Rock before plunging beneath the Pennsylvanian coal measures of southern Illinois.

Split Rock rises from the alluvial plane, and, like Buffalo Rock, is an island of sedimentary stone. In the cross section exposed by the split, the lines are visible, slanting skyward into the eroded vacancy of the valley; this rock is all that remains of a massive layer of sandstone that once lay a hundred feet thick across this valley, its substance reduced to silt and sand by glacial outwash and now buried beneath a thousand miles of Illinois and Mississippi river bottomland.

Surrounding Split Rock are fertile but inhospitable wetlands called the bottoms, the appearance of which has changed little since

1677 when Father Calude Allouez, Marquette's successor at the Kaskaskia mission, wrote of the "multitude of swamps which render the atmosphere unhealthy, and often covered with fog—giving rise to much sickness and frequent peals of thunder."[3] During canal construction, swamps like this spawned swarms of mosquitos, a constant source of "fever and ague" for the workers. Plates 43, 44, and 45, which illustrate the bottoms, were all taken within a few steps of the towpath.

The canal route, to a much greater extent than that of the later railroad, was determined by the lay of the land. Besides the expected mechanical and logistical problems in large construction projects, the canal engineers had to deal with the physical attributes of water: its enormous weight, the energy required to change its level, and the effort to contain large volumes within a hundred-mile ditch.

The canal bed at this point had to be high enough to avoid becoming mired in the lowlands, and low enough to maintain the correct fall from the Fox River aqueduct to the river level at La Salle. Unfortunately, a plug of solid sandstone (plate 46) lay directly across the only possible route and was probably the single most challenging obstacle to canal construction. The engineers had no alternative but to split the rock by cutting a water gap straight through.

The photograph of the southern outlier of the split (plate 46) was taken from the top of its northern counterpart. Beyond the rock, to the south, is the slough fed by Pecumsaugan Creek as it drifts toward its confluence with the Illinois River. A dam constructed in the 1920s across the creek has formed Split Rock Lake, seen in the upper right. The far bluffs are the southern bank of the ancient outwash channel whose swirls and eddies are preserved in the patterns of erosion around the uncut edges of Split Rock. The Illinois River flows behind the faint delineation below the horizon, and from the rock I can see tugboats, their stacks flashing white as they glide behind the green pickets of the trees.

During the 1890s, an interurban track spanned the canal, and its trestle rested in the notch cut from the left side of the rock. The train passengers could relax under a pavilion built on this rock and watch the canal boats pass below. But since the canal closed and the great "interurban era" ended, this rock can be reached only by the towpath.

[3]Thwaites, *Travels and Explorations*, vol. 60, p. 161.

From my vantage point 150 feet above the canal, I am at summit level: the vertical drop below me represents the fall of the canal from Chicago to the Illinois River. I scan the horizon through the camera, then point it to the west: the clear sky reflects from the surface of the canal, rifle-metal blue aimed straight toward La Salle. A jogger is coming down the path heading east back toward Utica, and I follow him in the ground glass of the camera. As he passes below me, the rhythmic thwack-thwack of his sneakers on the gravel echoes from the sheer face of the split across the canal. His shadow forms grotesque silhouettes that follow in the hollows of the rock. He disappears beneath the trees overhanging the towpath, leaving me alone, and I turn back to the lowlands lying across the valley floor.

This is one of the fullest panoramas of the corridor, and in the face across the canal I imagine the folds of its history, leaving tracings in layers like the Shakopee strata. The land, we believe, reveals itself the same to us all, but in truth we each view it from our own perspective, shaped by our times and tempered by necessity.

Marquette looked with appreciation on the landscape, but his was a geography of the spirit. La Salle also wrote eloquently of the Illinois and Mississippi valleys, but he and his fellow voyageurs were driven primarily by adventurism and aggrandizement. To the fur traders, its value was in its yield of pelts. The fertility of the soil, the stands of timber, and the power in the rapids attracted the American settlers, and the interest of the canal builders and engineers ran no deeper than the six-foot depth of the prism. The merchants saw the corridor as a trade route, and industrial entrepreneurs disregarded (and discarded) the landscape entirely in favor of the minerals buried below it. The tribes of the Illinois, perhaps, came closest to accepting the land in its wholeness, incorporating its streams, wildlife, and hills into their worldview as well as their economy.

As the sun sets, I watch the darks and lights contend for the surface of the stone across the canal. My rendering of the breadth and depth of this narrow strip of land is also selective and incomplete; the texture of this stone, and the landscape, is finer than the camera can record. After years of travel and research in a land we think of as "barren," Barry Lopez could still write, in *Arctic Dreams*, that "whatever evaluation we finally make of a stretch of land, no matter how profound or accurate, we will find it inade-

64

quate. The land retains an identity of its own, still deeper and more subtle than we can know."[4]

The complexity Lopez speaks of is not only in the landscape but resides also in our minds. It is in our need to form connections between things past and present in our world, those intricate bonds, strong as sinews, but delicate and elusive as spider webs, which reveal themselves differently in varied slants of light. There is texture within texture, layer upon layer—nowhere does it end with a blank surface upon which all is rendered; there is always more detail beyond.

[4]Barry Lopez, *Arctic Dreams* (New York: Scribners, 1986), p. 228.

Photographs

1. Lock 2 chamber, looking west, west of Lockport. *Middle Division, Mile 30, El. 570 ft. (10 ft. below lake level), Lift 10 ft.*

2. Lock 2, north wall, tail bay, west of Lockport. *Middle Division, Mile 30, El. 570 ft. (10 ft. below lake level), Lift 10 ft.*

3. The Chicago Portage. This photograph of the Des Plaines River is at the approximate point of the old portage.

4. The canal between Utica and La Salle. *Western Division, Mile 92, El. 471 ft. (109 ft. below lake level)*

5. The I&M Canal at midsummer, between Utica and La Salle. *Western Division, Mile 93, El. 471 ft. (109 ft. below lake level)*

6. The canal, looking east, in the Gebhard Woods State Park, Morris. *Middle Division, Mile 58, El. 514 ft. (84 ft. below lake level)*

7. Unocal Oil Refinery, near Lemont. In the foreground is the Chicago Sanitary and Ship Canal; beyond the railroad tracks is the Des Plaines River. The canal runs among the trees between the river and the refinery.

8. Lockport pumping station of the Wolverine Pipeline Company. Refineries and storage "tank farms" line the upper reaches of the corridor. Through this station gasoline, heating oil, and diesel fuel from refineries in the corridor are pumped to Detroit.

9. Tank farm near the site of the Chicago Portage

10. Tank farm near the site of the Chicago Portage

11. Brandon Lock on the Illinois Waterway, Joliet. A few yards to the east of the dam, beneath the trees on the left, is Lock 5 of the I&M Canal. The standard width of the locks on the Illinois Waterway is 110 feet, the exact length of the old canal chambers.

12. Lock 10, Marseilles. The chamber wall on the left was restored by the Civilian Conservation Corps in the 1930s. *Western Division, Mile 74, El. 500 ft. (80 ft. below lake level), Lift 8 ft.*

13. Lock 9, Marseilles, showing anchor irons and lower (downstream) wing wall. *Western Division, Mile 74, El. 508 ft. (72 ft. below lake level), Lift 8 ft.*

14. Lock 14, La Salle, looking west. The inner chamber is 110 feet long by 18 feet wide. The floor of the chamber was originally covered with oak planking. Just above the gate is the site of Lock 15, and beyond is the steamboat basin where river boats docked. *Western Division, Mile 96, El. 451 ft. (129 ft. below lake level), Lift 14 ft.*

15. Lock 14, chamber and mitre gate, La Salle. All gates closed pointing upstream, against a mitre sill of timber on the bottom of the chamber. *Western Division, Mile 96, El. 451 ft. (129 ft. below lake level), Lift 14 ft.*

16. Lock 14, gate detail, showing heavy balance beam, La Salle. Extending to the upper left is the smaller lever for operating the butterfly valve in the gate. *Western Division, Mile 96, El. 451 ft. (129 ft. below lake level), Lift 14 ft.*

17. Aqueduct over the Little Vermillion River, La Salle. *Western Division, Mile 95, El. 465 ft. (115 ft. below lake level)*

18. Fox River Aqueduct, looking east, Ottawa. Its seven original piers, constructed of Joliet limestone, remain, but the superstructure, originally of timber, has been replaced by an iron trough. *Western Division, Mile 81, El. 491 ft. (89 ft. below lake level)*

19. Aqueduct over Aux Sable Creek, Grundy County. *Middle Division, Mile 52, El. 514 ft. (66 ft. below lake level)*

20. Railroad bed following the canal right-of-way at the mouth of Pecumsaugan Canyon, looking east, between La Salle and Utica. *Western Division, Mile 93, El. 465 ft. (115 ft. below lake level)*

21. Looking southwest from the Kingery Road bridge. The abandoned prism of the canal is obscured by the foliage between the utility poles and the junkyard. *Summit Division, Mile 17, El. 588 ft. (8 ft. above lake level)*

22. Illinois Central Railroad trestle, across the canal, near La Salle

23. Iron ring for docking canal boats on the Norton Building, Lockport. The warehouse, built in 1849 by Hiram Norton of locally quarried limestone, was one of many stone warehouses built along the canal.

24. St. Patrick's Church, La Salle. This church has walls of white Joliet limestone and was the first stone church in La Salle County. The architect, Father Patrick Mullaney, had worked on the canal, and the labor was largely donated by canal workers who would show up from all down the "line" in gangs, led by their canal bosses, driving oxen and draft houses, and carrying picks and shovels.

25. Restored barn probably used to house canal mules, adjacent to the side cut, Ottawa. The canal was thirty feet above the Fox River at Ottawa. The engineers took advantage of this drop by digging a lateral canal, or "side cut," which diverted water from the canal to supply mills and factories with hydraulic power.

26. House on the canal bank, La Salle. Because the state still owns most of the canal right-of-way, the land is made available on ninety-nine-year lease terms for home construction.

27. Canal-era facades, Canal Street, Lemont

28. Gaylord Building, Lockport. This building has stood on the canal bank in Lockport for 150 years, one of the few having survived, more or less intact, the depredations of developers and fire and the ravages of nature. The central portion, with the low arches, was built in 1838 for storing canal construction equipment. After the canal opened, the building was used as a grain warehouse, and has since been occupied by a lock factory, a printing plant, and a plumbing supply company.

In 1984, the canal route was declared a National Heritage Corridor, and the Gaylord Building was designated as its anchor facility. It contains an information center, a restaurant, and galleries of the Illinois State Museum. The Gaylord Building stands as a symbol of the significance of the canal and of the commitment to its preservation.

29. Reddick Mansion, Ottawa. In the local history of every canal town are found biographies of its notable figures, often founders of an industry around which the community coalesced. They were usually first-generation Americans, many drawn from the East by the freer economic environment of the frontier.

William Reddick is illustrative of these civic forebears. In 1835, he and his wife moved from the East and bought a farm in La Salle County. Three years later he was elected county sheriff and moved to Ottawa, the county seat. For twenty years he operated a dry goods and grocery store there, and served as a state senator for eight. He was involved in education, both at a local and state level, and was on the board of directors of several local businesses. But his fortune was made in real estate, and in 1855 he had this mansion built, where he lived until his death in 1885. It was left to the city of Ottawa and is now a national historic landmark.

30. The "Halfway House," between Joliet and Chicago on the Old Stage Road. It is located on the Illinois River near the site of the great "Illinois village, Kaskaskia," referred to in the writings of Marquette, La Salle, and others.

31. Grain elevator, Seneca. Built in 1862 and the oldest remaining elevator along the canal, it is of heavy timber post-and-beam construction with a limestone foundation. The elevator was powered by steam, and its system of pulleys, buckets, and belts could lift three thousand bushels of grain an hour. From here, grain was shipped by canal to Chicago, and from there by boat over the Great Lakes or by rail to eastern markets.

32. Canal-era barn, Dresden

33. St. James Sag Church, Mount Forest Island

34. St. James Sag Cemetery, Mount Forest Island

35. Père Marquette monument, Summit. The plaque reads:

Father Marquette landed here
1675
This monument is constructed of boulders
brought
by the glacier from the Lake Superior region and deposited
in this valley having traversed the route later followed
by the earlier French explorers La Salle, Joliet, and Father Marquette.
Erected by Chicago and Alton Railroad Company
August, 1895

PÈRE MARQUETTE
BORN AT LAON FRANCE JUNE 1 1637 HE DIED NEAR
LUDINGTON MICHIGAN MAY 18 1675
EVOTED MISSIONER AND HEROIC PRIEST-EXPLORER
E OFFERED THE HOLY SACRIFICE OF THE MASS NEAR
THIS SPOT MAUNDY THURSDAY AND EASTER SUNDAY 1675
AND ESTABLISHED THE FIRST CHRISTIAN MISSION IN
THE ILLINOIS COUNTRY
THIS MONUMENT ERECTED UNDER
ARCHBISHOP JOSEPH H. SCHLARMAN BISHOP OF PEORIA
BY THE CONTRIBUTIONS OF MANY WAS UNVEILED BY
HIS EMINENCE SAMUEL CARDINAL STRI
BISHOP OF CHICAGO SUNDAY OCTOBER 14

36. Père Marquette monument, Utica

37. Towpath, near DuPage River slackwater crossing, Channahon. *Middle Division, Mile 44, El. 518 ft. (62 ft. below lake level)*

38. Strip mine tailings, Buffalo Rock

39. Cog Hill Golf Course. The Chicago-Joliet Road follows the north bluff of the old Chicago Outlet. Along the ridge of the bluff, overlooking the quarries and gravel pits, are the rolling fairways of Cog Hill Country Club built in the 1920s among the uplands of the Valparaiso moraine. Glaciers left similar terrain in Scotland, and in the late nineteenth century that terrain inspired the invention of golf. The construction of a golf course usually requires the reconfiguration of the land to a morainal terrain, but here the gently dimpled landscape was used as it was found. Nowhere is the contrast of land use in the corridor more apparent than here, where the beauty of the surface landscape prevails along the ridge, while just below it has been scarred irrecoverably by strip mining.

40. Gravel quarry, near Utica

41. Limestone kiln ruins, Blackball Mines, near Utica

42. Limestone kiln ruins, Blackball Mines, near Utica

43. The "bottoms," along the canal, near La Salle

44. Carey Marsh, Illinois River bottomlands north of the canal, near Utica

45. The "bottoms," taken from the canal towpath, looking north toward the Illinois River

46. Split Rock, the canal, and its towpath, looking southwest. *Western Division, Mile 94, El. 451 ft. (129 ft. below lake level)*

JIM REDD, a data processing consultant living in Chicago, is a native of Birmingham, Alabama. He received a B.S. in mathematics and physics from Samford University and a B.A. in anthropology and linguistics from the University of Alabama. His photography has been exhibited in galleries throughout Chicago and has been published in many books and articles.